Common

Meet Jesus

by Knofel Staton

You may obtain a 128-page leader's guide to accompany this paperback. Order number 40093 from Standard Publishing or your local supplier.

New Life BOOKS™

A Division of Standard Publishing
Cincinnati, Ohio 45231
No. 40092

Scripture quotations are from the New American
Standard Version unless otherwise noted.

© 1980, The STANDARD PUBLISHING Co.,
division of STANDEX INTERNATIONAL Corp.

Library of Congress Catalog No. 80-53674
ISBN: 0-87239-426-3

Printed in U.S.A.   1980

To

the first teacher who caused the life of Jesus to come alive for me. Largely because of his teaching, I am what I am—and teach and write the way I do today.

Dr. Marion Henderson

In appreciation of:

my wife, Julia
who typed and edited the first draft from my handwriting, which seems to be getting worse as the years pass.

and

Mrs. Nancy Presko
who untiringly and encouragingly typed the final manuscript.

Table of Contents

one

His Heredity—Our Hope

Matthew 1; Luke 1:26-38; 3:23-38

Do you know your pedigree? Are you proud of your genealogy? If you would investigate your family's past, I wonder how many skeletons you would find in your closet. I imagine many of us would just as soon some of the facts about ancestors would remain buried.

James Farmer tells about a wealthy woman who hired an author to write her biography. The author discovered that one of her grandfathers had died in the electric chair at Sing Sing. The woman wanted that information so written that the black spot in her family's past would not be obvious. So the author put the facts together in this way: "Her grandfather occupied the chair of electricity in one of America's most noted institutions. He was very much attached to his position and literally died in the harness."

Jesus' genealogy had a few black spots in it, but Jesus did not ask His biographers to hide them. He was not ashamed to make public His human pedigree, and this suggests that He will never be ashamed of His present or future family tree, which can include you and me if we are not ashamed of Him (Mark 8:38). The fact that He did not seek to erase some of the names from His genealogy is proof to us that He is not interested in erasing our names from the book of life just because we are not perfect. We should not think that we are too bad for Jesus to accept us as His kin or to publicly admit His relationship to us.

His Human Pedigree

Jesus' genealogy appears in two places—Matthew 1:1-17 and Luke 3:23-38. The two lists are not the same, for Luke traced Jesus' family through Mary and Matthew traced it through Joseph. In these two lists we find hope for the entire human race.

For the benefit of the Jews, Matthew traced Jesus' ancestry back to Abraham (Matthew 1:1). A true-blue Jew must be able to trace his roots back to Abraham, the father of all the Jews (John 8:33). Genealogical lists occur routinely in the Old Testament. Part of the Jewish hope that the Messiah would be their eternal high priest rested upon His connection to Abraham, to whom God had said, "In your descendants all the nations of the earth shall be blessed" (Genesis 22:18).

But Jesus' family tree also contained hope for all non-Jews. Luke traced Jesus' ancestry *beyond* Abraham through Noah (Luke 3:36), the father of all humanity after the flood, and back to Adam (3:38), the father of all humanity before the flood, and on back to God (3:38), the Creator of every nation of mankind (Acts 17:26). There is no way to lock Jesus into being the Savior for just one ethnic group of people. His heredity crossed all human groups, and He intends for His presence to be with all human groups today. Jesus is for all races and situations.

Of course the big question is about us. Are we as open and extensive as Jesus is? His commission to us is to make disciples of all the nations (Matthew 28:19). The Greek word for nations *(ethnos)* is the basis of our word *ethnic*. Jesus was not talking about geographical boundaries only: He was talking about crossing all ethnic barriers with the gospel. If we would cover every corner of the earth's surface but make disciples only of the white people, we would not be carrying out Jesus' commission.

Jesus is for both the Jews and the Gentiles, and those two groups include all the people on earth. But what about the hopeless and godless sinners in each one of these groups? Jesus does not turn His back on them, does not bar them from leaving their sin and entering His family, just as He did not hide the godless sinners in His family tree.

One of the Jewish leaders in Jesus' genealogy led God's people to do more evil than all the surrounding pagan nations were doing—Manasseh (Matthew 1:10; 2 Kings 21:1, 2, 10, 11). Rehoboam acted so selfishly and sinfully that the united people of God were split into two groups (Matthew 1:7, 1 Kings 12:1-16).

Remarkable in Jesus' family tree is the inclusion of four women—Tamar, Rahab, Ruth, and Bathsheba (Matthew 1:3-6). If you could select four Old Testament women to be in your family tree, whom would you choose: Sarah, Hannah, Deborah, Esther? I doubt that you would choose a harlot or an adulteress, but such women were in Jesus' ancestry.

Two of the women, Rahab and Ruth, were not even Jews. Ruth was a Moabite, one of a nation of people whose enmity barred them from the "assembly of the Lord" (Deuteronomy 23:3). Rahab belonged to a pagan nation and lived in Jericho. If she signed in on the program "What's My Line?" how would she register? As a harlot, a prostitute!

Tamar was no jewel, either. She tricked her father-in-law into a sexual liason and gave birth to twin boys as the result (Genesis 38:12-18, 27-30). Bathsheba committed adultery with her neighbor while her husband was away serving his country in the military. Realizing that the resultant pregnancy could not be attributed to her husband, the neighbor (David) arranged to have her husband killed in battle.

The presence of these people in Jesus' family tree may be taken as a symbol of the great truth that in Jesus all barriers are broken down—the barriers between male and female, between Jew and Gentile, between sinners and upright people. All people need God's grace, and in Jesus God's grace is greater than any of man's circumstances. There is no reason for anyone to shy away from Jesus because of his or her family or because of his or her own past life. Jesus came to close the door to our past and to open the door to our future with Him. He can cleanse us from all our sin.

If Jesus would not admit His kinship with the Gentiles, the women, and the sinners among His ancestors, it might be hard for us to think He would overlook our imperfections and sins. But we can call Him Savior, for He came to save His people from their sins (Matthew 1:21). Luke 3:23-38 shows that he is related to all the descendants of Adam, and He offers salvation to all of them.

His Divine Pedigree

Jesus is our Savior not only because of His human pedigree, but also because of His divine roots. Jesus' birth was unique, just as His existence was unique. Jesus did not begin His existence at Mary's conception or at the time of His birth in Bethlehem. He existed with God from the beginning (John 1:1). He existed before any created thing existed: "He is before all things, and in Him all things hold together" (Colossians 1:17). Matthew traces His lineage to Abraham, but Jesus stated that He existed before Abraham (John 8:58). Jesus shared in the creation of the world:

All things came into being through Him; and apart from Him nothing came into being that has come into being (John 1:3).

For in Him all things were created, both in the heavens and on earth, visible and invisible, whether thrones or dominions or rulers or authorities—all things have been created through Him and for Him (Colossians 1:16).

In Jesus' prayer to God in John 17, He spoke about the glory He had with the Father before the world existed (v. 5). As God the Father is eternal, so is Jesus the Son eternal. In fact, Jesus is called the first and last (Revelation 1:17).

Though born of the virgin Mary, Jesus existed before Mary did. In fact, He was the Creator of Mary. He came to live for a time in the human body that was formed in Mary's womb.

Of course we don't understand the "how" of it any more than Mary did. But the angel's word is still the best answer: "For nothing will be impossible with God" (Luke 1:37).

It was no human being, no physical substance, no material thing that caused Mary to conceive. It was the Holy Spirit of God (Luke 1:35; Matthew 1:20). Jesus therefore was called the Son of God (Luke 1:35), and He called God His Father (John 17:1). Even Jesus' worst enemies knew this meant He was divine (John 3:18). God sent Jesus, who lived with Him not only before He was born in Bethlehem, but also before the world came into being (John 17:5).

Some scholars like to question the virgin conception because only Matthew and Luke record anything about it. If such a miraculous event had really happened, they say, it would have been known to Mark and John and Paul.

However, the fact of the virgin conception is very plain in Matthew and Luke. There would be no reason to doubt these records even if it were true that other writers did not know about it. But the other writers certainly did not write down all they knew (John 20:30). The fact that they did not mention the virgin conception does not indicate that they did not know about it.

Mark began his record with the ministry of John the Baptist. Since he did not record Jesus' birth at all, he did not have occasion to mention the miraculous conception. But note how carefully Mark mentions "the son of Mary" in telling what the neighbors in Nazareth said (Mark 6:3). Some neighbors said "the carpenter's son" (Matthew 13:55). Matthew quoted that without stopping to explain that Jesus was not really the son of the carpenter, Joseph, because Matthew had already made it clear that Jesus was the Son of God. But Mark had not recorded the miraculous conception. If he had quoted the neighbors' opinion that Jesus was the carpenter's son, some readers might think it was true. Knowing that Jesus was not the son of Joseph, Mark carefully quoted "the son of Mary."

And did John know about the miraculous conception? He wrote, "The Word became flesh, and dwelt among us." It seems plain that he knew Jesus did not come into the world by an ordinary birth.

And did Paul know about the miraculous conception? It is very clear that he knew Jesus was God's Son, that God sent Him, that He had lived with God before, and that He had had a part in creation (Romans 1:3, 4; 8:3; Philippians 2:5-8; Colossians 1:16, 17). There surely is no reason to think he did not know the truth about Jesus' conception.

Jesus experienced a natural birth after a super-natural conception. Without the virgin conception, He would have been mere man or wholly spirit; through the action of the Holy Spirit and the virgin, He was God-man. The miraculous conception was God's means of executing the incarnation, the process of coming into flesh. The pre-existent Jesus (John 1:1) became flesh (John 1:14) by taking the form of a human (Philippians 2:6, 7) in the womb of Mary (Matthew 1:21; Galatians 4:4).

Our Hope

If Jesus were merely man, we could have no eternal hope in Him. A man could have people of many kinds in his family tree and be able to cross all barriers between people, but only Jesus can point also to a divine family tree, to His conception by the Holy Spirit.

We can have hope in Jesus because of His divine nature. The Holy Spirit not only brought about His conception, but also was with Him throughout His service on earth.

1. The Holy Spirit gives divine power (Acts 1:8), and Jesus showed such power (Matthew 11:5).

2. The Holy Spirit and Jesus worked together in creation (Genesis 1:2; John 1:3), and Jesus on earth was able to create—He multiplied fish and bread before people's eyes (Matthew 14:15-20).

3. The Holy Spirit is the Spirit of truth (John 14:16, 17), and Jesus' words were true, even though the religious leaders did not believe them (John 8:45).

4. The Holy Spirit convicts men of sin (John 16:8), and Jesus turned the spotlight on the sins of people around Him (John 8:44).

5. The Holy Spirit is *holy,* and Jesus was pure and totally trustworthy.

6. The Holy Spirit unites men to men, and so does Jesus (Ephesians 2:11-22).

7. The Holy Spirit provides diversity in unity (1 Corinthians 12), and Jesus surrounded himself with people who differed and yet were united in following Him.

8. The Holy Spirit is the seal of God's ownership (Ephesians 1:13, 14), and Jesus spoke and acted as one owned by God (John 12:49).

9. The Holy Spirit works the re-creation of a person (John 3:5, 6), and Jesus brought God's re-creating activity to earth so man could be remade in the likeness of God (2 Corinthians 5:17).

10. The Holy Spirit is the presence of God himself (Psalm 139:7), and the presence of Jesus was the presence of God in human flesh. To watch Jesus in action was to watch God in action. "I and the Father are one" (John 10:30). No wonder the angel declared Jesus to be Immanuel, God with us (Matthew 1:23).

When we see Jesus feed the hungry, touch the untouchables, love the unlovables, forgive the sinners, raise the dead, overcome Satan and death, and can realize that He is not just man, but He is both God and man—then we can hope! We can know that God is not only *with* us, but He is also *for* us. What good news that is! And that is the gospel that deserves to be received, proclaimed, and practiced.

two

The Surprises of the First Christmas

Luke 1:26-38; 2:1-20

Christmas is a very special holiday for the majority of us. The soft and joyous music filling the house, the beautiful tree with wrapped gifts beneath it, the holly and mistletoe, the smells of baking, the noise of family fun, the parties, the special programs, the stacks of Christmas cards, the pushing crowds in the stores— all are precious parts of Christmas. And we especially love the surprises of Christmas—the opening of packages, the unexpected expressions of love and happiness, the friends who drop in to share our joy.

The surprises that surrounded that holy night so many years ago—the night often called the first Christmas—are so magnificent that none of us can fully comprehend their significance. We can ponder about them for a lifetime and never exhaust their magnitude nor fathom their depth. Every time I meditate upon the events of that first Christmas, I become like the small lad who takes his pail to the beach but realizes there is no way he can get the entire ocean into it.

Surprise 1—The Father and a Couple of Youngsters

Whom would the Heavenly Father trust with His most valued treasure? A mature, married, wealthy, experienced couple? No, He chose a couple of poor nobodies, a young couple engaged but not yet married, perhaps teenagers.

The Bible gives no definite information about the age of Joseph and Mary. It seems, however, that Jewish people usually married young, and there is no reason to think these two were an exception. It is quite generally supposed that Mary was a girl in her teens.

Some suggest that Joseph was much older and died while Jesus was still a lad, but we have no solid evidence to substantiate that. The supposition rests on the fact that Joseph is not mentioned in the Gospels after the record of his trip to Jerusalem when Jesus was twelve years old (Luke 2:41-51). Jesus' mother and brothers come into the story at later times (John 2:12; Mark 3:32), but not Joseph. But even if Joseph died before Jesus was thirty years of age, that does not prove anything about Joseph's age. Some people die young even in our age of medical marvels, and in ancient times even more died without reaching old age.

We cannot help admiring this young couple. Both of them exhibited a fine devotion and willingness to let God have His way regardless of the cost.

Mary had much to lose by becoming pregnant before marriage. Who would believe her story of an angel? Everyone would scoff at her claim that the Holy Spirit made her pregnant with no physical contact. How could she make Joseph believe she was still a virgin? How could she convince her parents that she had done nothing wrong? How could she face her friends in the youth group at the synagogue? Some time later, probably with inspiration from the Holy

14

Spirit, she could say, "All generations will count me blessed" (Luke 1:48); but in the near future she would be more likely to be maligned than blessed. But the word of the angel was surely the message of God, so Mary said, "Be it done to me according to your word" (Luke 1:38).

In her agitation Mary hurried off for a long visit with her elderly cousin Elizabeth. Their fellowship and the inspired messages must have done much to encourage her—but still she had to go back and face Joseph, her parents, her friends, the whole town of Nazareth.

Joseph proved to be a noble character. Understandably, he did not buy Mary's story about the Holy Spirit making her pregnant. Who ever heard of such a thing? He must have thought she had been unfaithful and had made up an incredible lie besides. Still he was not vindictive or spiteful. He did not want to punish her with humiliation or public disgrace. He had to divorce her, he thought, for in those days the engagement rather than the wedding was the legally binding contract. But good-hearted Joseph intended to keep the matter as private as possible. Then came the angel's message, and Joseph promptly accepted both the message and Mary.

As the time came near for the baby to be born, the couple must have talked about the trip that had to be made to Bethelehem, a trip of ninety miles. Joseph had to be registered at the birthplace of his ancestors, but could Mary make such a trip? It would take three days. Could she bear to walk or ride a donkey for that distance? Did God direct her to go? Was Joseph concerned about the wagging tongues in Nazareth? We don't know their thinking; we just know they made the trip together.

Enroute to Bethlehem, did Mary and Joseph talk about the coming Messiah and the new covenant He would usher in? If they passed close to Bethel, did they compare Jacob's dream with their own? If they crossed the Jordan where their forefathers crossed over into the promised land, did they speak of the Messiah and the new and eternal promised land where Mary's Son would reign? We are not told of their conversation, but the marvelous message of the angel to both of them must have been much in their minds.

Amid all the movement and excitement of the political and economic arena of that day—oppressive military government, marching demonstrations, and crooked businessmen—the spotlight falls upon a poor, quiet, and religious young couple. They waved no flags. They burned no census cards. They identified with no rebellions. Yet around them something happened that changed the course of the entire world. They were then unknown, but now they cannot be forgotten.

God made somebodies out of nobodies, and He does the same today. The Christian's body becomes the home of God's Spirit (1 Corinthians 6:19, 20). In the church that is Christ's body, nobody is a nobody.

Surprise 2—The Master in a Manger

At last the travelers came to Bethlehem. Even Joseph was tired, and Mary must have been exhausted. But they were not the only strangers there. If there was more than one inn, the "no vacancy" signs were out everywhere. "There was no room for them in the inn."

The record says nothing of an innkeeper, but as we think of the story we like to imagine one. Often we make him a villain, but I imagine him differently. I think it is time we got off his back. I think he was a nice man; I think he did all he could for the tired-out travelers.

Inns in those days were wild and noisy places. Public bazaars, the butchering of animals, the marketing of wine and meat, drinking, and the noise of reveling through the night were commonplace. I think the inn-keeper was not a scrooge nor an angry isolationist; he did not scream "No room! Get moving!"

No, I think he saw Mary's condition and had com-passion. He knew the couple needed a quiet place; but there was an overflow crowd, and no private rooms were available. He knew Mary should not sit among the revelers in the public patio all night. So he thought of a quiet, private place where the crowds would not bother—not the bustling place where travelers kept their camels and donkeys, but a stable somewhere near.

I think he did not send them to a filthy, stinking barn. Animals were well taken care of in those days; they were as important to their owners as our automobiles are to us. A stable can be as clean as a garage.

I am not suggesting that it was the Holiday Inn either. God's Son from Heaven did not demand the best of earth. He did not ask for a mink-lined bassi-nette or pink and blue baby clothes. All he needed was a place to sleep. He owned the cattle on a thousand hills, and He was willing to make their feeding trough His bed.

As a baby in Bethelehem he needed to be comforted and rocked, but later He would do the comforting. Soon He babbled and cooed, but later He spoke the most meaningful and purposeful words known to mankind. Then He needed quietness, but afterward He needed to be heard by the multitudes. He was content at one time to sleep in a manger, but now He is seek-ing for men and women in whom He can live. In people He has moved from the boundaries of the manger to the ends of the earth. The innkeeper did not know who Jesus was, but we do. Or do we? Do we save any room for Him in our lives? The synagogues had no room for Him. The Sanhedrin had no room for Him. His hometown had no room for Him. The only place He found undisputed room was on the cross!

Surprise 3—The Creator of Man and the Keepers of Animals

The Creator of the earth (John 1:3) was going to visit the earth, and who were the first to know? The kings and queens? No, Herod and Augustus had not even the foggiest idea that anything unusual was happening. The news media of the first century? No, not even the Barbara Walters of the day got an interview. The Jerusalem Gazette didn't have a reporter on the scene.

The King of kings was born, and who were the first to know? Some insignificant itinerants out on the hillside (Luke 2:8-10). Those who were looking after the lambs were the first to look upon the Lamb of God.

The great King David was once a shepherd; but by the first century, respect for shepherds had taken a downward slide. They were among the lowest class of people; they were migrants who ate and slept with the animals—and smelled like them, too. They displeased the rabbis by being often awol from the religious services.

God did not send His concert of angels to this overlooked group of humans by accident. When no one else cared about them or wanted to associate with them, God's angels penetrated the midnight clear with the positive message, "There has been born for you a Savior" (Luke 2:11). For whom? For the outcast. For the neglected. For the poor. For the despised. For the shepherds, "the Savior is born." A new day was coming, a day of "peace among men" (Luke 2:14). To the humblest, God announced the highest. To the poorest, God announced the richest.

The shepherds give us our first example of what to do when we hear the good news of Jesus. They left their activities to approach Jesus. They weren't content with a report about Him; they wanted to be in the presence of the Savior. They came in *haste.* No procrastinating. No making of excuses. The Savior demanded their priority (Luke 2:15, 16).

After being in the presence of Jesus, they proclaimed Him (Luke 2:17). The first human preachers of the Messiah preached without attending one day of classes in a Bible college. They were not concerned about whether they had philosophy down pat or whether they knew all the technicalities of grammar. They only knew they had met the Savior and had to tell about Him. It made no difference that they were looked down upon by the masses; they had to tell what God had done.

Many times God has used some of the most unlikely people to do His bidding. He puts His treasure in earthen vessels (2 Corinthians 4:7). He is not a respecter of persons. All He needs are people who have come to Jesus and are willing to go and tell others. The humble shepherds caused the people to wonder (Luke 2:18).

Then the shepherds returned to their vocation and responsibilities. Jesus does not call for us to drop out of society. These men went back to their "Monday" job after having a "Sunday" with Jesus. But on their "Monday" jobs, they were different men. They went into the fields rejoicing and honoring God (Luke 2:20). They had changed so much that I am sure the sheep sensed it.

About You

Christmas can hold no significant surprises for you unless a change takes place in your life—a change caused by Jesus. Jesus must move out of the manger and find lodging in your mind and heart. Then you will be able to sing, "Glory to God in the highest, and on earth peace among men" (Luke 2:14).

three

The Scrapbook of Memories

Luke 1:5-25, 39-80; 2:8-52

The Shepherds

Mary was a young girl who gave birth to a baby boy far away from home. She did not have the help of her mother or a midwife. But she did not fear, for she knew she was a part of God's plan. Just as she was settling down to rest after the arduous experience of giving birth, she heard the sound of men's voices outside the stable. She heard footsteps amidst the other night sounds. Joseph came in then and said they were to have visitors. Visitors? Yes, they want to see the baby.

Strange men entered the stable, excitedly telling about their unusual experience in the fields. Then they hushed as they knelt in awe in front of the baby. Their visit was a very special and precious memory, one of the many that Mary began to place into the scrapbook of her heart: "Mary treasured up all these things, pondering them in her heart" (Luke 2:19).

Even after the shepherds left, Mary probably lay awake considering the significance of their visit and thinking about all that had come to pass. She no doubt watched the sleeping baby in the manger and began to sort out all of her feelings and thoughts. Thinking back to that time several months ago, she could hear what the angel had said to her, and then she recalled what the prophets of old had said about her and the baby.

She had been called the mother of the Lord (Luke 1:43). The child she had just given birth to was Christ the Lord, the Messiah! The long-awaited Savior had come! And she and Joseph would be responsible for Him! What a moment for remembering!

Zacharias and Elizabeth

Mary's thoughts may have dwelt long on the three months she had spent with Elizabeth and Zacharias. She remembered the joy and the wonder her aged relatives had felt.

Zacharias was one of about twenty thousand priests in Palestine. Twice a year he went to Jerusalem to participate in a week's priestly service in the temple. Each priest dreamed of the day when he would be chosen to perform the highest duty—the burning of incense. It was such an honor! Only one priest could perform it at a time—and only once in his lifetime. How excited he must have been as he entered the temple to perform the highest duty of his profession! (Luke 1:8-10).

The crowds outside began to get concerned. Zacharias had been in the temple for a long time (Luke 1:21). "Do you suppose he became ill? He is quite old, you know," the people probably murmured. Finally he came out. But he looked strange. The people tried to converse with him, but he could not speak. Whatever happened? He had received quite a surprise. An angel had appeared to him and told him he and his wife would have a son even in their old age (Luke 1:11-15).

And a very special son he would be! He would be named John and would turn people to the Lord (Luke 1:13, 16); he would be called the prophet of the Most High (1:76); he would be like the great prophet Elijah (1:17); he would prepare the way for the Messiah (1:76).

How excited yet how humbled Zacharias and Elizabeth felt to have such an important part in God's plan! How they must have thought back to the experience of Abraham and Sarah, and felt themselves likewise privileged! And how joyful Elizabeth was that at last she would have a child! Elizabeth was six months along when Mary came to visit. How thrilled Elizabeth was to learn that Mary was carrying the Savior in her womb! "Mary, when you came near, my baby leaped inside my womb for joy because the mother of the Lord has come to me" (Luke 1:44, my paraphrase).

Home in Bethlehem

Evidently soon after Jesus' birth, Joseph began looking for a place to live and a job in Bethlehem. We do not know why they decided not to return to Nazareth. Perhaps the folks back home had never accepted the story about the miraculous conception and had given the couple a hard time—or possibly Joseph and Mary had not even tried to tell the story they knew would not be believed. We note later that the unbelief of the people of Nazareth prevented Jesus from doing miracles there (Matthew 13:54-58).

Joseph's trade was marketable in any village or city. He was a builder. A carpenter was one who was skilled in woodworking, including repair work and original construction of houses, furniture, utensils, and agricultural implements. Joseph was in the manufacturing business.

We do not know when Joseph and Mary moved from the stable, but we see that they were living in a house when Wise-men from the East came to greet the Savior (Matthew 2:11). That was more than forty days after Jesus was born, and it may have been months later than that. There were two other notable events before the coming of the Wise-men.

The Circumcision

Joseph and Mary were in a strange town, far from the influence of their parents and the hometown synagogue, but that made no difference. The eighth day arrived, and they knew that according to God's law their son had to be circumcised (Genesis 17:12; Leviticus 12:3). The event is recorded in just one small sentence (Luke 2:21), but the implications are mountainous.

Circumcision identified a person with the nation of Israel and with the covenant God had made with the ancient forefathers. Circumcision communicated commitment. When parents had a son circumcised, they were dedicating that son to become a covenant man. They were also dedicating themselves to raise the boy so he would become a man of the law. Jesus would be reared to know, respect, and obey God's Word. He would be the first human to completely fulfill the law (Matthew 5:17), and through Him God would offer the world a new covenant (Hebrews 12:24), which would require circumcision not of the flesh, but of the heart (Romans 2:29; Philippians 3:3; Galatians 6:15).

Our world would be a much better place if every young couple away from the home folks and the home church would remain dedicated to their religion. How great it would be if all parents would seek to rear children committed to God! Too many keep putting off religious training. The children are infants—but soon they are walking, then riding bicycles, then driving cars. Before the parents realize it, the children are out on their own—and what about the time that was lost, the time they did not spend in the study of the Christian faith? Can it ever be made up?

When Jesus was thirty years old, He attended the services at the synagogue "as was His custom" (Luke 4:16). This is not surprising, since the custom of attending was begun when He was only a week old. Mary never shirked her responsibility with the excuse that she could not get anything out of the service because of a wiggling baby. Mary and Joseph attended regularly, partially *because of* the baby, not *in spite of* Him. They never thought about letting their children decide for themselves about attending worship services. They made public the decision for God when Jesus was just eight days old.

Parenting children involves far more than the reproduction process. Flowers and weeds can reproduce. Mice and men can reproduce. But real parenting involves much more. It involves dedication and commitment. It involves time and effort. We can't take what we own with us when we die, but in all likelihood we will have our children with us in eternity. Where we will be depends on our own dedication and our parenting.

The Temple

Thirty-three days after the circumcision of Jesus, Joseph and Mary entered with the baby into the court of the temple at Jerusalem (six miles from Bethlehem) to fulfill other responsibilities. The law of Moses outlines two special rituals that were to be adhered to after the birth of a son: (1) the purification of the mother (Leviticus 12), and (2) the presentation of the child to God (Exodus 13:2).

The purification was a ritual cleansing of the mother following the birth of a child. It was to be accompanied by an offering of a one-year-old lamb and a young pigeon (Leviticus 12:6). But God allowed the poor to substitute another pigeon for the lamb (Leviticus 12:8). The price for the offerings was placed in trumpet-shaped containers (thirteen of them were located in the court of women). The third one was for the use of the poor and was called "the offering of the poor."

Mary went to the third container and dropped in the price of two young pigeons (Luke 2:24). Jesus' earthly parents were poor materially. They lived humbly; as Joseph's trade increased, so did their family (Mark 6:3). Jesus knew from first-hand experience that God provides daily necessities (Matthew 6:19-34).

Jesus never allowed His poverty to destroy His self-image. Neither did He spend time brooding about things He did not have. In reality, He had great riches. He had the love of His earthly parents. They provided for His needs, protected Him, reared Him to love and respect God as well as His fellowmen, encouraged Him to develop into a balanced person. After the purification ceremony had ended, Mary could participate in the redemption of the firstborn (Numbers 18:15, 16; Luke 2:22b-23). This ceremony involved presenting the firstborn son to the priest in recognition of God's ownership, and paying five shekels to redeem him. This ceremony literally offered the firstborn to God, who in His graciousness gave the child back to the parents to care for and protect.

But the experience was not over yet; Mary would receive still more memories to store in her heart. While many people in Israel were looking for a military Messiah who would lead a violent revolution against Rome, there were others who did not look for such a confrontation but for "consolation of Israel." Simeon was of this latter group. Prompted by the Holy Spirit, he declared that in Jesus he had seen God's salvation not only for Israel, but also for all nations (Luke 2:25-

32). In the same hour, a female prophet named Anna offered thanks to God and spoke about God's redemption of Israel (Luke 2:36-38). It was a full and wonderful day in the temple of the Lord.

The Threat

Herod ordered a mass murder of infants in order to insure Jesus' death. Joseph and Mary left their house and job in order to protect Jesus. After the threat was over, they returned home to Nazareth (Matthew 2:13-23).

The Silence

Luke records Jesus' visit to the temple at the age of twelve, but we read nothing else about His youth except summary statements of His development (Luke 2:40-52).

This obscurity has been overshadowed by the mark He left as a man. He re-oriented life on this whole planet. He didn't travel more than 175 miles from His birthplace, but news of Him has spread worldwide. The date of His birth is the basis of our calendars. He has changed more lives than anyone else.

Napoleon once said, "I know men, and I can tell that Jesus Christ was no *mere* man. Between Him and every other person in the world there is no possible term of comparison."

Mary's memories would have added, "Amen."

four

The Campaign Manager

Matthew 3:1, 2; Mark 1:1-7; Luke 3:1-18; John 1:19-34

He was campaign manager for the most recent candidate for king, but he did not wine and dine the elite. He did not organize dinners at a hundred dollars a plate. He made no political promises and engaged in no under-the-table deals. He accepted no interviews with the mass media. And when special interest groups clamored for his attention, he sent them away with the message that they had better clean up their act. What candidate could survive a front man like that? Jesus, that's who.

Jesus' kingship continues today and will continue forever. He has changed the course of humanity. He does what John the Baptist, His campaign manager and press agent, said He would do: He "takes away the sin of the world" (John 1:29), grants the Holy Spirit to believers, and grants punishment to non-believers (Matthew 3:11, 12). And His kingdom is just as John described it—the kingdom of heaven (Matthew 3:2).

There was no fighting in their campaign headquarters, for Jesus and John agreed. Jesus even echoed

John's words at times (Mark 1:14, 15). There was no credibility gap; there were no petty jealousies plaguing their plans. While John pointed out the superiority of Jesus (Matthew 3:11; Mark 1:7; Luke 3:16; and John 1:27), Jesus bragged about the greatness of John (Matthew 11:11).

The prophets had been silent for four hundred years, but Malachi's final words told of the new prophetic day that would come (Malachi 4:5, 6). And the new age was ushered in by John the Baptist, the "Elijah" of whom Malachi spoke (Matthew 11:14)

John's Servitude

Any visit of a king in the first century was preceded by a forerunner and herald whose job it was to smooth the road on which the king would ride. The forerunner would remove the stones, smooth the lumps, and fill in the holes. In that day the path was made ready and was straightened for the king's comfort and convenience. The forerunner was also a messenger who heralded the impending arrival of the king. He would travel through the villages saying, "The king is coming! The king is coming!"

John was the forerunner and herald for Jesus, but he was not interested in smoothing literal paths. He was interested in getting people ready to receive the King. He did not look for stones in the roads, but in the hearts of men. Instead of smoothing the lumps and filling in the crevices, he humbled the proud and exalted the humiliated (Luke 3:5-14).

John was a master in the art of persuasive speech. He had a magnetic manner and personality. Crowds thronged to hear him speak. He had the people eating out of his hands. He could say "Jump!" and they would answer, "How high?" He had great power; he could motivate the masses. But John still was a humble, submissive servant. He could have had a powerful position or riches, but instead he had himself under God's control.

John the Baptist was just the opposite of the Hitlers, the Jim Joneses, and the Moons of history. He claimed nothing and took nothing for himself. He didn't even take up love offerings or make heart-rending appeals. His bank account did not grow one bit, even as the crowds grew larger and larger. He never demanded first-class accommodations; he never charged fees for his seminars. John had committed himself to the Master instead of trying to act as the master of others.

John was the kind of servant that Paul mentioned in 1 Corinthians 4:1—a *huperetes,* which means literally "an under-rower." This type of servant sat under the deck of the ship manning the oars and getting no credit, while the captain received the praise for the swift smoothness of the ship's course. But the under-rower did not mind, for he was rowing for the satisfaction of the captain. That was John's attitude—he was preaching and baptizing for the captain of the ship.

One of the most remarkable evidences of this attitude is recorded in John 1:37. People heard *John* and followed *Jesus.* Two of John's disciples immediately became Jesus' disciples. It's not every preacher who is happy when two of his supporters begin to support another preacher. We all can learn much from John's servant attitude.

John had no wish to elevate his status. Some seemed willing to give him a fancy title (John 1:21), but he refused to accept it. He wanted to be known only as a "voice" (John 1:23). He was joyously secure in being a humble servant of the exalted Savior. Every Gospel writer quoted John as saying, "I am not worthy to untie His sandals" (Matthew 3:11, Mark 1:7; Luke 3:16; John 1:27). In those days, people wore open-toed sandals on the dusty roads. When they would enter into a residence, the lowliest slaves would untie the sandals of the travelers. John said that in comparison to Jesus he was not even equal to this kind of household servant. John was interested in service, not status; for this attitude Christ praised him (Matthew 11:7-10). Jesus would later encourage James and John to have this attitude (Matthew 20:26, 27). And at the last supper, the Master himself would set an example of a serving attitude (John 13:3-16).

John's Courage

John was humble, but he was not timid. He was not a soft-soaper or an ear-tickler. He saw the issues and needs of the day (even though he looked and lived like a hermit) and spoke about them regardless of his audience.

He was a prophet, not a politician. When the political leader of his day was living in sin, John publicly pointed the finger of accusation at him. He not only preached against Herod's marrying his brother's wife, but he also exposed "all the wicked things which Herod had done" (Luke 3:19). John could not have held a special religious service in the "White House" of his day without calling for the moral turnabout of the politicians from the top down. John evidently believed that "righteousness exalts a nation, but sin is a disgrace to any people" (Proverbs 14:34).

Positive results come when preachers do not bypass the political arena when calling for repentance. Some have been executed for speaking out for the right, but their influence has far outlived the negative influence of the executioners. We must learn that sin is a cancerous boomerang. When hurled it comes back to hurt the one who threw it. Sin is an infestation; if we do not seek to cut it out of our leaders and officials, it will spread to the whole nation. If we don't have the courage of John and try to eliminate sin with the antiseptic of the gospel, then sin may destroy us.

John's Message

About repentance. The most significantly progressive periods in history have come out of religious revivals. The Reformation in Europe and the Great Awakening in America were seeded in revivals. Revivals should never be considered outmoded.

Revivals are most effective when they are first of all directed to the insiders—the people of God. The classic revival message comes from Isaiah:

> Come now, and let us reason together, ...
> though your sins are as scarlet, they will be as
> white as snow; though they are red like crimson,
> they will be like wool.   —Isaiah 1:18.

This was a message to those who were already the people of God (Isaiah 1:1).

God sent John the Baptist to those who were known as God's people, and John called for their repentance. As long as the situation within the church is similar to the situation within Judaism in John's day, revivals are needed. A revival within the church is needed before evangelistic programs to reach into the world can get off the ground. An inner revival must always precede an outer reformation.

John's audience included people of all the interest groups within Judaism. The Pharisees were the legalists who evaluated a person's religiosity by his fulfillment of the written law and the handed-down oral tradition. The Sadducees were pro-government; they wished to protect the status quo so that government regulations would not be imposed upon Judaism. They differed doctrinally with the Pharisees over the resurrection and angels. The Zealots were anti-government; they thought that rebelling against Rome was the way to bring in God's kingdom. And to them all, John said "Repent."

31

John did not allow himself to be lured into any special interest group or its topics of discussion. He preached only Jesus, who was superior, eternal, and the Lord. He did not speak about hobbyhorses or doctrines or traditions. He did not allow different issues and questions to detour his main message. He knew that the central issue must be Jesus and the people's reception of Him.

About smugness. The Jews thought they had a monopoly on salvation. With the right God, the right Scriptures, the right place to worship, the right doctrines, etc., they felt they "had it made." After all, their heritage could be traced to Abraham. They loved to drop the names of their ancestors in their conversations. They were so smug in their security that they taught that Abraham sat at the gate of Hell to detour and deliver any Jew who might show up at the wrong gate.

John pulled their security blanket right out from under them when he said, "God is able from these stones to raise up children to Abraham (Matthew 3:9). He was saying God could make Jews out of dead stones! And he went on to say that if they did not produce fruit, they would be thrown into the unquenchable fire (Matthew 3:10, 12).

Does your Christian group draw a circle around itself and think God's salvation is to be experienced only within that circle? Can people be saved even if they never join *your* church? Beware of smugness.

About day-to-day living. When John called for repentance, the Jews were puzzled. "What do we need to repent of?" they asked (Luke 3:10). Then John dropped the bombshell. He said God's kind of religion is not lived out in the synagogue and the temple only. It must get out into the streets, marketplaces, and homes. God's religion affects a man's social and business dealings (Luke 3:11-14).

This message was called the gospel (Luke 3:18) because it was good news to hear that God's religion is not to be divorced from the day-to-day activities of life. Jesus would change a man wherever he is and whatever he is doing—not just in the place of worhsip.

Nowhere should the kingdom of God be more visible than where we work all day long and where we live all year long. There is no way we can get by with serving God one day a week and ripping off or mistreating our fellowmen six days a week.

About insincerity. John did not tolerate the intentions of some people who came to hear him just because it was the most popular happening of the time; "You brood of vipers, who warned you to flee from the wrath to come" (Luke 3:7). John did not in any way give those people a false sense of security.

When do we offer a false sense of security? When we allow baptism without repentance (Luke 3:7, 8), when we accept repentance without any change of conduct (3:8), and when we accept either baptism or repentance without a confessing of sins (Matthew 3:6; Mark 1:5). We must sincerely admit to ourselves the sins we are committing. Only then will we recognize a need for a Savior. Only then will we know that we are insufficient by ourselves. Only then will we sincerely confess Jesus and actually allow Him to be Lord of our lives. And only then will Jesus confess His relationship to us before the Father (Matthew 10:32).

Summary

John the Baptist unveiled the Savior of the world by preaching about sin, repentance, confession, and baptism. The same topics are involved in preaching the gospel today. To proclaim God's message continually is to be in a continual revival, and to ignore it is to regress into smug, superior, and insincere religiosity.

five

The Waiting Is Over

Matthew 3:13-17; Mark 1:9-11;
Luke 3:21-23; John 1:32-34

Hurry up and wait! How many of you like to wait? I don't know of anyone who does. Ever notice how fidgety we become as we wait in our cars behind a long line of cars at the drive-in bank or with our cart behind a long line of carts in the supermarket?

America as a nation is on the go. We Christians also have caught the go-aholic fever. We think we always have to be in motion. We race against deadlines that we establish ourselves. Often there is no one else in the race, but we push our human accelerators to the floor and put our gears in high. We cannot stand to let our human engines idle or our gears be in neutral.

The Waiting Game

God has often called on His people to wait. Joseph in the Old Testament knew he was going to be used by God; he even dreamed about it. But it did not happen all at once. He had to wait many years and endure some mistreatment and agony before God's plan through him came to fruition.

Moses was chosen by God to do a certain task, but he had to wait eighty years before God was ready to use him. The apostles had just seen the risen Lord; they were champing at the bit to take over the world for Christ. They were at the starting post ready for the gates to open. But Jesus gave them a tough commandment—wait (Acts 1:4). They did not have the slightest hint as to how long they would have to wait, but the right time finally came.

Men often get impatient with God's timetable and launch out on their own. Joseph tried to force his family to accept his leadership by telling them about his dreams that they would bow down to him. But such talk got Joseph into trouble.

Moses got tired of waiting and launched out on his own, trying to show his people that he was their leader. But his action only resulted in his banishment from his people.

There must have been times when Jesus wanted to start His ministry. Since the age of twelve (and perhaps earlier) He had known that He was to do the business of His Heavenly Father. But days, months, and years went by as He remained at the business of His foster father, Joseph the carpenter. Christ probably wondered from time to time how much longer He would be known as simply a carpenter.

People were lonely; the sick were dying; the Gentiles were being mistreated; sins were multiplying. Yet Jesus was not to move to relieve their distress. He must have walked by crippled children and asked God, "Now, Father, now?" But Jesus was not impulsive. He knew that God would select the right time—and that time would be the best time. So Jesus waited and waited and waited.

However, the years of waiting were not wasted. Jesus soaked up many experiences that later found form in His illustrations as He taught. He knew what it meant to be yoked together. He knew the hearts of the rich and the cries of the poor. He knew how women put leaven in a piece of dough and why they did not sew new patches on old clothes. He watched what happened when new wine was stored in old wineskins. He had seen the transformation of a small mustard seed. He knew about roots, vines, branches, and fruit. He knew about planting, and how weeds grow up with the good plants. He knew what happened during the sowing of seed, and how it was scattered onto different types of soil. He knew how crooked a furrow would get if the farmer looked back. He was at home with businessmen, for He knew about a baker's bread, a jeweler's pearl, a writer's words, a candlemaker's light, a fisherman's fish, a builder's foundation. He was aware of what was going on.

But when Jesus' time came, He quit taking orders to do custom-made carpentry. He completed the jobs He had promised, hung up His tools, tidied up His work area, and slid His stool underneath the work bench. When Jesus' time came, He was ready to do the Father's bidding. When His time came, He was willing to walk three days to the Jordan River to see John the Baptist.

The Baptism—the Beginning

Jesus could hardly see John at first. The crowds were dense and full of motion. Often those who were moved by John's preaching stepped toward the river bank, admitted their sins, and were immersed. John had promised that the day of the Messiah was just around the corner and warned them that their hearts had better be ready.

Jesus listened to John's preaching, but He did not just listen. He got involved. His total person became involved, not just His ears. Jesus could have "amened" every sentence of John' sermons and said, "Preach on, John! Give it to them, John!" and thought to himself, "This is not for me. He is asking for repentance. I have nothing for which to repent. He is calling for confession for sins. I have committed no sins. He is asking for baptism. If there is anything I don't need, it's baptism. Why should I go through such humiliation for nothing? He's not preaching for me—but preach on, John!"

But Jesus did not think that way. He did not waver. He had no fancy excuses, although from a man's standpoint He was the only one there with a legitimate reason not to be immersed. God had a reason, however, for asking Jesus to submit himself in such a way. Consider the five reasons that follow. Can you think of others?

To fulfill righteousness. John was was shocked when he saw Jesus emerge out of the crowd to be immersed in the Jordan. At first he even refused to baptize Jesus (Matthew 3:14). But Jesus would not allow a refusal: "Permit it at this time; for in this way it is fitting for us to fulfill all righteousness" (Matthew 3:15).

What did Jesus mean by fulfilling all righteousness? The Greek word for righteousness was originally used to refer to the quality of conforming to a given standard—of obeying the rules. Righteousness is the quality of being and doing what is right in accordance with the regulations. A person is righteous when he does what God says to do.

Jesus was baptized as an act of righteousness in response to God's command for Him to do so. Jesus came to do His Father's will, not His own (John 6:38). He said and did what His Father told Him to do (John 12:49). For Jesus, it was not *my* will but *thy* will (Matthew 26:39).

It is easy to reverse that to *my* will be done, not *your* will. And many times that reversal is seen right at the point at baptism. To submit to immersion is a humiliating act. And it gets tougher if no one else in the family has done it. We often think the religious traditions of our parents and grandparents should be good enough for us; we need not look further. But rationalization is not a synonym for righteousness. Obedience to God's wishes is the way of righteousness. We can get so caught up in the theological systems that belittle baptism that we neglect God's command to be baptized. We must not neglect a command of God for the sake of the traditions of men (Mark 7:8).

If the perfect man, Jesus, submitted to baptism in order to fulfill righteousness, then we who are imperfect ought to do it also.

To be identified. Besides fulfilling righteousness, Jesus' baptism was a means of identifying Him. He was identified both in the realm of Heaven and in the realm of earth.

Since John's baptism was from Heaven (Matthew 21:25) and since Jesus was from Heaven (1 Corinthians 15:47), He was aligned with a Heavenly act in baptism. God honored that alignment by identifying Jesus as His Son (Matthew 3:17). When we are baptized, we also identify ourselves with Heaven; for we are raised with Christ (Romans 6:4), we are clothed with Christ (Galatians 3:27), and we are alive together with Christ (Colossians 2:13).

Jesus was also identified with the earth in His baptism. He who had emptied himself by putting on human flesh (Philippians 2:7; John 1:14) now identified with human flesh by submitting to baptism.

Jesus was not a lone ranger. Although He never sinned, He stood in line to identify himself as a friend of sinners. Since baptism is a symbol of death and burial (Romans 6:3, 4), Jesus was giving a sneak preview of the fact that He would later identify with the sinners by a voluntary death and burial in their stead.

When we are baptized, we too identify ourselves with all sinners who need God's grace. To refuse baptism is to proudly stand on the bank as if we were not like those sinners. If the perfect Jesus could identify with mankind, then surely we who are imperfect can do so also. To submit to baptism is to confess that we have sinned and are willing to die to our old life-styles and bury our past in order to begin new lives.

To be installed. John emphasized that the kingdom of God was at hand, but every kingdom needs a king. God publicly installed Jesus as that king when Jesus was baptized. God made the installation speech himself when He declared, "This is My beloved Son, in whom I am well pleased" (Matthew 3:17). See the prophetic declaration in Psalm 2:6-9.

The surprise was in the kind of king Jesus would be. God combined Psalm 2:7 with Isaiah 42:1 when He said, "In whom I am well pleased." The Isaiah passage is speaking about a servant, not a king. But that is the paradox—Jesus was to be both a servant and a king.

How different! A king who stressed service, not status; a king who stressed others, not self; a king who was willing to die for the sake of His people— what a wonderful king Jesus would be!

To receive power. How would Jesus convince people that He, a lowly carpenter, was the true king? God gave Jesus power to do signs and wonders that would verify His kingship (Acts 2:22). This special anointing of Jesus happened when the Holy Spirit descended upon Jesus at His baptism (Acts 10:38). This does not mean that Jesus did not have the indwelling presence of the Holy Spirit—He was conceived by the Holy Spirit. But in this day God granted to the human Jesus the power of the Spirit to do miracles. Up to this time, Jesus had done no miracles.

The baptism identified Him as God's anointed to John the Baptist (John 1:32-34), and His work following this day would identify Him to others (John 2:11; Acts 2:22). For the first time in Jewish history, a king would function in accordance with God's ideal of what a king should be (1 Samuel 12:13, 14). He would truly be called the King of kings and Lord of lords (Revelation 19:16).

To initiate the ministry. Jesus' baptism also initiated His ministry (Luke 3:23). His miracles were to accompany His ministry. His signs were to verify His status: "The works that I do in My Father's name, these bear witness of Me" (John 10:25).

But what kind of ministry would He really live out? He had the power to move mountains, but He was still human. He could still succumb to human temptations to misuse that power and to rely on His status. Nowhere is a man's character tested more than by observing how He uses great power and status. Power can turn inward; it can hurt, wound, and destroy. Jesus is the King with great power. How will He use it?

Read on.

six

He Would Not Be Moved

Matthew 4:1-11; Mark 1:12, 13; Luke 4:1-13

Are you on the inside what you seem to be on the outside? When the outer wrappings are removed from the package of your life, what remains? When the outward mask is removed, what does your inner face look like? When you are through playing games, what realities are there to face you? What makes you tick?

Inner Selves

Who we are on the inside is greatly determined by our *goals.* We will change the direction of our lives, enter into difficult experiences, and be willing to pay a lot of money if our goals can be achieved in these ways. Many will endure years of schooling to reach the goal of a chosen career. Goals motivate us to "stick to it" even when the way gets rough.

But goals alone do not decide our inner selves; our personal *values* determine how we go about reaching the goals. Our values are dominating inner forces of our characters. In all of our activities we are realizing our values as we pursue our goals.

Both our goals and our values have great power, and at time they wage a battle within us. If our goals are more powerful than our values, we may be willing to violate our values in order to reach our goals. One may believe in honesty and integrity but violate those values in order to pass a course that is important to his goal or in order to get a job promotion. But if a person's values are more important to him than his goals, he may make a change in his goals in order to remain honest and pure. When we are emotionally healthy, we keep our goals and values in a good balance. When we are spiritually healthy, we make certain both our goals and our values square with God's will.

Our goals and values formulate our character; they are the essence of our motivations. They determine how we use our *abilities.* God has given to each Christian some type of ability to do certain ministries. Each ability represents some sort of power to function meaningfully and selflessly in the body of Christ (2 Timothy 1:7; Romans 12:4-6; 1 Corinthians 12:4-7). Some can influence others with their words. Some can organize; some have the power of charm; some show power in their acts of mercy. Some can influence others with their abilities in music.

God intends that we use these gifts for the good of others, not to build up ourselves (1 Corinthians 12:7; 1 Peter 4:10, 11). But Satan tries to lure us into using our abilities wrongly. He knows the best way to make us sin is to change our goals and values by putting self ahead of others.

Immediately after Jesus was installed as the King, Satan stepped in (Mark 1:12, 13). He used many clever tricks to persuade Jesus to change His goals and values so He would use His abilities for self-gratification rather than for others. We can learn from Jesus' experiences the tricks that Satan uses and how to meet those temptations with power and victory.

I am reminded of my football career. As a freshman in high school, I decided I wanted to be a pro football star. I was so enthusiastic and excited that first day of practice! I gloried in catching passes and running around would-be tacklers. I felt I was a great success already. But then the coach told us to lie down. For the next forty-five minutes, we did push-ups, scissor kicks, sit-ups, and other types of strenuous exercises.

My football career began *and* ended on that day. I failed to see that those exercises had anything to do with winning games. They were painful, not pleasant. I wanted to play, not work. So I took off my uniform and never returned. I let the stress test flunk me.

But Jesus faced up to the "tests" and won the victory by refusing to give up God's goal and values. He would not be moved to go Satan's way. We too can gain the victory by remaining committed to God's purposes and goals, by using our God-given abilities for the service of others, and by not violating God's values that should be an intrinsic part of us.

seven

Trouble in the Hometown

Luke 4:16-30

Time seemed to fly after Jesus cleaned off His work bench, put up His carpentry tools, and started toward Jordan to participate in John's revival. Nearly a year later He came back to Nazareth. He had started the journey alone, but now a group of students had been traveling with Him—Andrew, Peter, Philip, Nathanael, and probably John and James (John 1:35-51). He had been one of many carpenters, but now people were voluntarily calling Him the Savior of the world (John 4:42). Once unknown except in Nazareth, He now was famous. Through some months in Judea people had thronged about Him, attracted by miracles He did (John 2:23). Now in Galilee they were doing the same (John 4:45).

He had turned water into wine at a wedding (John 2:1-11); He had courageously driven the con men out of the temple (John 2:13-25). He had discussed God's will with a Jewish ruler (John 3:1-21), and with a half-breed woman of Samaria (John 4:1-26). He had seen an entire village come out to Him and beg Him to stay with them (John 4:28-30, 40-42). He had spoken to the highest and the lowest of society, performed miracles, and been recognized as the Messiah—but now He was back home. How would His hometown people receive Him?

Back Home Again

Hometown folks are a strange lot. They help shape a boy's character; they remember all about him and his family. They enjoy bragging about the boy who made good, and they point to his picture with pride. But if he comes back to speak to them or point out to them some areas in which they need to improve, they turn a deaf ear. Suddenly the hometown boy feels terribly lonely among people whom he thought were his friends.

Jesus knew about this tendency, and His heart probably skipped a few beats as He began to notice the familiar landmarks—the curve in the road, certain trees, and the homes of children with whom He had played as a child. Jesus was no doubt wondering how the hometown folks and the hometown synagogue would receive Him. He loved the people so much. He did not want them to miss out on what He was doing elsewhere. Maybe they would ask Him to speak in the synagogue service!

As Luke records, it was Jesus' custom to go to the synagogue on the Sabbath (Luke 4:16). He had gone every week as He was growing up; and even though He had left home, He had never abandoned the custom. He never got the idea that He was too good to mingle with the people in the synagogue, even though He was perfect and many of them were hypocrites. He listened to sinners exhort others about how to live, even though He knew all the answers about God's will and living it out. He did not quit listening when others spoke, even though He knew much more than they did. Whenever we get to thinking we are too smart or too good to attend the local church regularly, we should remember Jesus and His attitude.

The Service

The service in the synagogue probably began as usual with the words of the worship leader: "Blessed are thou, O Lord, our God, King of the world, former of light and creator of darkness, author of welfare and creator of all things." Then came the reciting of the *Shema:* "Hear, O Israel! The Lord is our God, the Lord is one! And you shall love the Lord your God with all your heart and with all your soul and with all your might" (Deuteronomy 6:4, 5). The service always gave God the center place of adoration and worship.

A series of prayers followed the *Shema.* The prayers began with praise to God and ended with thanksgiving to God intertwined with six established petitions, each of which was followed by the congregation's saying together, "Blessed are thou, O Lord."

Then a male was selected and invited to read a portion of Scripture from the first five books of the Old Testament. Another male was selected and asked to read from the prophets. On this occasion, Jesus was the hometown boy who had made good; He was asked to read a selection from the prophets.

The Sermon

Jesus turned to the text He wanted His hometown relatives and friends to hear. He wanted the text to outline some of the characteristics of the new kingdom that God was inaugurating through Him. He wanted to give the hometown folks a glimpse of what His ministry was all about. He chose a text from Isaiah:

The spirit of the Lord is upon Me, because He anointed Me to preach the gospel to the poor.

He sent Me to proclaim release to the captives,
and recovery of sight to the blind, to set free
those who are downtrodden, to proclaim the
favorable year of the Lord.   —Luke 4:18, 19

As was the custom, after reading the text, Jesus sat
down to give a brief homily or exposition drawn from
the Scripture. All eyes were fixed upon Him. The
hometown folks were wondering what He would say.
Jesus began by saying what no other person had ever
been able to say about that text, "Today this Scripture
has been fulfilled in your hearing" (Luke 4:21). The
people did not understand either the text or the statement about its fulfillment, but they were surprised and
pleased by His gracious speaking. Wonderingly they
asked, "Is this not Joseph's son?" (Luke 4:22).

Jesus knew they did not understand, and He anticipated that what He had to say next would not be well
received (Luke 4:23, 24). The admiration of the
hometown folks would soon turn to antagonism, for
He was going to tell them the truth.

The text of Isaiah was not clear to the worshipers
because they had always read it with their blinders on.
For centuries they had spiritualized that text; they had
made the Bible fit their preconceived ideas, rather
than letting the Scripture change their ideas.

The rabbis taught that people were poor or sick because of God's disfavor. They looked down on the
handicapped and underprivileged as well as the Gentiles, the females, and the immoral. The religious elite
did not give people in these categories the slightest
hint that God loved them.

When faced with references to the poor, the blind,
the downtrodden in the text in Isaiah, the religious
leaders said these meant the spiritually poor rather
than the literally poor, the spiritually immature rather
than the literally blind, the Jews mistreated by Romans

rather than the Gentiles mistreated by Jews. The teachers read the text, they memorized it, they preached from it; but they never took one step toward ending the social woes around them or toward erasing the stigma of certain categories of people. They missed the whole point of God's will for them as individuals and as a nation.

But Jesus was God in the flesh, and He came to make known God's character and will (John 1:14, 18; 2 Corinthians 5:19). He came to reach out to the despised, the neglected, the downtrodden. He came to show God's love for the poor, the sick, those who were fractured in body and spirit, and those who had been stepped on socially for generations. The "favorable year of the Lord" was the time when God's grace and care would be for people of all classes, regardless of ethnic background, poverty, or physical disability.

Jesus came to tear down the fences that the Jews had built between people. He would demonstrate that God is no respecter of persons, that He treats Jew and Gentile, young and old, male and female, and rich and poor alike. Jesus was going to stand up to the pride, the prejudices, and the narrow-mindedness of the Jews.

In His sermon to the hometown synagogue, Jesus dropped the bombshell of the nature of His mission. He made clear that God's compassion and loving care are universal—for anybody and everybody who will appreciate and accept them. To illustrate His point, He used two examples from Jewish history recorded in 1 and 2 Kings.

In the day of Elijah, a great famine hit Israel and other nations. Instead of giving relief to any of the "chosen people," God helped a poor Gentile widow (Luke 4:26; 1 Kings 17:9-24). She was in several categories the Jewish teachers would call "wrong"— she was poor, a Gentile, and a woman. No ordinary

Jew would care a thing about her. But Jesus pointed out that God cared. God supplied her with an in-exhaustible amount of food and enabled Elijah to bring her son back to life.

Before that example and its implications could sink in, Jesus gave another illustration. During the time of Elisha, God did not cure any Jew of leprosy; but He did cure a Syrian soldier (Luke 4:27; 2 Kings 5:1-14). The Jews despised Syrians, and especially Syrian soldiers. Jesus' reminder that God's love extended to such out-casts was like pouring a box of salt on open wounds.

The Rejection

The hometown folks were no longer wondering about Jesus' words or misunderstanding His meaning. They got His message loud and clear, and they did not like it one bit—to put it mildly. Luke said it this way: "And all in the synagogue were filled with rage as they heard these things" (Luke 4:28).

Instead of receiving the hometown boy and rejoic-ing with Him in His message and mission, they re-jected Him altogether. Not one person stood at the door to shake His hand or commend Him for a job well done. Not one family invited Him home for a dinner. Instead they wanted to get rid of Him, and they couldn't seem to do it quite fast enough for their lik-ing. They not only threw Him out of the synagogue; they also threw Him out of the city and tried to kill Him by throwing Him off the hill on which the city was built (Luke 4:29).

Thus Jesus was rejected by the people who should have loved Him most. We can learn from His experi-ence how people may react when their lifelong preju-dices are challenged. Jesus promised His disciples that people would treat them in the same way that He had been treated if they would continue to preach His truth and carry on His mission (John 15:20).

We as Christians are citizens of Jesus' kingdom, and we need to live out our citizenship by following His commands and example. We should be breaking down the fences that divide people. We should be telling and showing the love that God has for all persons, regardless of IQ, color, nationality, political affiliation, or size of one's bank account.

Jesus was crucified for His stand. Stephen was stoned because He said that God was bigger than the Jewish nation and could not be held in the Jewish temple (Acts 7). The first strong controversy in early Christianity arose because the Gentiles had been accepted as Christians (Acts 15). Yes, it is difficult to speak out against prejudices, and it may take years for any progress to be noted.

Jesus is demanding a lot from us. He does not want us just to study His words in neighborhood Bible studies or just to preach weekly about them. He wants His words and principles to be lived out in our everyday lives, to be in our every thought, and to be seen in our attitudes.

We can cast Jesus out just as the hometown folks did by ignoring what He said and refusing to put it into practice in our lives. But regardless of what we do, His kingdom will advance. Will we be a part of it by obedience, or will we risk being cast out ourselves on that Judgment Day that awaits all of us?

eight

The Friend of Sinners

Luke 5:1—6:11

No one enjoys rejection. Far away from the noisy, violent crowd of the hometown folks, Jesus no doubt sadly contemplated what had happened to Him. As He brushed the dust off His robe and looked back down the road to Nazareth, tears perhaps moistened His eyes. He probably felt quite lonely and dejected.

What should He do now? His own people had turned their backs on Him in violence and disbelief. Earlier Satan had tried to lure Him away from His mission with fantastic worldly treasures, and now His neighbors were saying in their rejection of Him that He should change His way of doing things and His plans for His ministry. Should He continue on this way that obviously was going to be very difficult? For a lesser man, the decision would have been extremely tough.

But Jesus could withstand rejection. He had come to earth to do God's will, not the wishes of men. He was committed to fulfill the law of the Creator, not the loves of the creatures. He had decided to perform God's principles, not to perpetuate man's prejudices.

God's truth, not man's traditions, must be proclaimed. Jesus had come to reveal to all what God is like; He could not do that by yielding to men's desires.

Isolation or Involvement

The Pharisees were the "separated ones" (the literal meaning of the word *Pharisees).* They were dogmatically concerned about law, righteousness, and holiness. Consequently their concept of God was limited. They thought of Him as the God of law, not love. They saw Him as one who gave rules to be obeyed, not as one who offered compassion. Their habits of life were filled with loathing rather than loving; they segregated themselves from sinners rather than serving them.

Some of the Pharisees were so concerned about keeping themselves separate that they would not even look at a sinner. One group was called the "bruised" Pharisees because they would close their eyes any time a female was within eyesight; they did not want to have evil thoughts. They would bump into trees, buildings, or chariots, because they were walking around with their eyes closed. They would rather be bruised and bleeding than look upon a sinner who might entice them to sin.

Jesus acted just the opposite. He talked and walked with sinners. He was entertained by sinners. He was involved, not isolated like the Pharisees; and He was criticized for it: "Why does your Teacher eat with the tax-gatherers and sinners?" (Matthew 9:11; Luke 5:30).

People had the idea that one would adopt the behavior and attitudes of those he associated with, so they claimed Jesus must be a drunkard and glutton (Matthew 11:19). The criticism did not stop Jesus' associations, however. His reputation was hurt, but He did not allow the prejudices of men to rule His life. He was much more concerned about keeping His character pure in the eyes of God than about having proper reputation in the eyes of the narrow-minded religious elite.

Now are we Christians isolationists, or do we get involved as Jesus did? Do the types of people who felt so comfortable in the presence of Jesus feel comfortable in the presence of church people today? It is clear that the people surrounding Jesus thought of Him as their friend before they saw Him as their Savior. We today cannot hope to draw people to Christ if we isolate ourselves from them.

A recent study in evangelism reveals that the longer a person is a Christian, the fewer people he brings to Christ. The most effective evangelists are those who have been Christians less than a year. The newer a Christian is, the more non-Christian friends he has whom he influences and introduces to the Savior. After being a Christian for a while, he loses contact with non-Christians.

We have convinced ourselves that if we associate with sinners, they will contaminate and ruin us. That is defeatism; we should be thinking victory! I grew up believing that sinners would contaminate me; so when I entered the military service and made friends with non-Christians, I got contaminated for a time. Why? Because I had been taught that would happen. I did not know I was a light that could cancel darkness; I thought darkness would snuff out light. I thought the evil one in the world was stronger than the One who lived in me. How wrong I was!

We in the church must prepare ourselves to associate with non-Christians and win them to Christ, not allowing them to win us away from Christ. We must learn from the methods of Jesus, not from those of the Pharisees.

Jesus maintained a balance between isolation and involvement. He often drew away from the crowds to be alone or to be with His disciples. See an example in Mark 6:31.

We must maintain that balance. We need to isolate ourselves from the world regularly in order to meet with fellow Christians and devote ourselves to "teaching, and to fellowship, to the breaking of bread, and to prayer" (Acts 2:42). We need to gather together to build up one another, admonish one another, discipline one another, pray for one another, and encourage one another so we can scatter into the world with the strength to touch those who are sin-sick without getting sin-sick ourselves.

Rituals or Responsibilities

Both the Pharisees and Saducees felt that rigorously-kept rituals would add up to righteousness. They watched like devouring hawks to catch Jesus breaking the rituals, so they could declare Him unrighteous. And they didn't have to wait long.

Strict Jews fasted on Thursday and on Monday. Evidently John the Baptist's disciples followed that man-made tradition, but Jesus' disciples did not. The law required only one fast a year, but men had augmented God's law with the idea that more fasts would increase their religious merit with God. They thought Jesus should do as they did.

Jesus answered their criticism by suggesting that He and His disciples were continuously participating in a wedding party and would not fast according to the customs (Luke 5:33, 34). The Jews accompanied their fasting with grim sorrow, but the presence of Jesus calls for joy.

Jesus did make it clear that there are times for sorrow and fasting, but those times arise from circumstances that bring sorrow. They are not to be written on our calendars and adhered to rigorously on set days (Luke 5:35). Jesus spoke of His kingdom as being entirely new, not tied to the old rituals. It is not the old kingdom with new ideas patched on. It is not to be bottled up in old rituals; it is to be really new! Keeping all the old rituals would ruin the spontaneity, the spirit, the compassion, the power, and the personal dimension of the new (Luke 5:36-39).

Christianity is not to be Judaism warmed over. If all we have is rituals, then we have nothing to help a world of needy, lost, and dying people. This is not to say we are to bypass the Christian rituals; it is to say that we must not allow rituals to detour us from our responsibilities to people.

It is possible to be so religion-scheduled that we have no time to be personally involved in the lives of others outside the meeting place—even our families may suffer. But it is also possible to be so busy serving that we neglect to worship God. We need the balance of worship and service. Jesus regularly attended the synagogue as well as the Jewish festivals, but He did not allow the multiplication of rituals to paralyze His ministries to others.

Sabbath or Service

The Jews worshiped a day as much as a deity. God said:

> Remember the sabbath day, to keep it holy. Six days you shall labor and do all your work, but the seventh day is a sabbath of the Lord your God; in it you shall not do any work, you or your son or your daughter, your male servant or your female servant or your cattle or your sojourner who stays with you. For in six days the Lord made the heavens and the earth, the sea and all that is in them, and rested on the seventh day; therefore the Lord blessed the sabbath day and made it holy.
> —Exodus 20:8-11

But the Jews added pages upon pages of ways to keep the Sabbath. To them these traditions carried as much weight as the original law of God.

The Sabbath began at sunset on Friday evening and was announced by three blasts of the trumpet. It lasted until sunset Saturday evening. The twenty-four-hour period was filled with more legalism than any other period in the Jewish life. A person's spirituality was evaluated by his strict observance of all the regulations governing the Sabbath.

But Jesus did not commit himself to everyone's expectations of Him concerning that particular day of the week. His disciples picked corn on the Sabbath (Luke 6:1, 2), and Jesus healed on the Sabbath (Luke 6:6-11; 13:10-17; 14:1-6).

One one occasion, religious leaders became indignant because Jesus healed a woman who had been doubled over for eighteen years (Luke 13:10-17). They preferred to let the woman suffer for another eighteen years rather than to allow Jesus to help her on the Sabbath. On another occasion, instead of seeing a crippled man made well, they saw only that their holy day was violated (John 5:1-18); and they continually persecuted Jesus because He did good on the Sabbath (John 5:16).

Jesus challenged their attitudes about the holy day (Luke 6:9; 13:15, 16; 14:5, 6). He shattered their concepts with three statements: (1) "The Sabbath was made for man, and not man for the Sabbath" (Mark 2:27); (2) "The Son of Man is lord of the Sabbath" (Luke 6:5); (3) "My Father is working until now, and I Myself am working" (John 5:17).

Jesus said even God himself worked on the Sabbath. That was really hard for the Jews to swallow. It was also hard for them to see how anyone could be the lord over the Sabbath, for to them the Sabbath was their lord during a paralyzing twenty-four hours. God did not create the Sabbath so the day would be served, but so man's need could be met. God did not intend for the day to be used against man and become a burden to him.

Paul taught that we should not judge one another by the observance of the Sabbath because that law was nailed to the cross (Romans 14:5, 6; Colossians 2:14-16.) We were freed from the law so that we can serve God with a new Spirit (Romans 7:6); yet this is not a freedom to do as we please, but the liberty to serve others with love (Galatians 5:13).

The Jews were wrong to rely so strongly on the observance of the Sabbath and to criticize Jesus, but this does not mean that we are to neglect meeting weekly with God's people (Hebrews 10:25). But we, on the other hand, are not to become so wrapped up in meetings that we neglect the needs of others. We must maintain a balance: we must worship God on a day (not worship the day) and be ready to serve anyone on *any* day.

Conclusion

Jesus broke old traditions and taught timeless principles; such action brought Him persecution and slander. But He also received popularity from the common people, for they understood at last that God cared for them and thought they were valuable persons. They experienced the good news they had been thirsting to hear. They found God to be a friend *and* a Savior!

nine

Jesus' Legacy

Mark 3:13-19; Luke 6:12-16

Have you ever thought about what you would do if the doctor told you that you only had a couple of years to live? It happens all the time, but few people are prepared for it. It is one thing to hear or read about it happening to someone else; it is quite another to be going through it yourself.

The main question is not when or why death will come. It is more important to consider what we will leave behind as a contribution to our fellowmen. Human life is like a relay race. One person runs awhile and before he quits he passes the baton to another person who carries it on. None of us should be satisfied to allow our thoughts, our concerns, our knowledge, our views, and our positions to fade away with us. We should pass them on.

Jesus had to do this kind of thinking. Even though He was at the height of His career, He knew He had come to die and would do so in less than two years. He wanted to make sure His mission and message did not die with Him. He wanted to plant and cultivate His

attitudes, beliefs, principles, dreams, ideas, and programs in others so they could carry on His message
and mission and fulfill God's intentions for man. But
how could He accomplish this task?

The Choosing

Many people followed Jesus everywhere He went.
They latched on to this great teacher and traveled with
Him, wanting to know Him as well as His teachings.
But Jesus was not satisfied with such a large, undefin-
able crowd. He wanted a "core group" in whom He
could invest more of himself. With a few disciples he
could monitor their progress and involve them closely
in what He was thinking, teaching, and doing. So early
in His second year of ministry He selected out of the
multitudes that followed Him twelve men who were to
be known as His apostles: "And when day came, He
called His disciples to Him; and chose twelve of them,
whom He also named as apostles" (Luke 6:13).

As we read about Jesus' choosing of these men we
can note several valuable principles.

1. Jesus did not ask the crowd to take a vote and
decide for Him who would be in that core group. He
knew He must do the choosing.

2. Jesus did not choose hastily. He waited for over a
year before selecting the apostles. If Jesus, who knew
all about men, took time, then perhaps we should not
be so hasty in choosing leaders for our new churches.
It takes time to know people and to see how they work
with others.

3. Jesus spent an entire night in prayer before
choosing (Luke 6:12). He did not depend entirely on
personalities or performances; He also depended on
God's direction.

4. Jesus did not choose "yes men"; He chose men
who would think, wonder, and challenge. He wanted
men who could act on their own and teach others.

5. He did not select men who were replicas of each other. They all had different personalities and different abilities. The strengths of some would complement the weaknesses of others.

6. Jesus did not select men on the basis of their accomplishments only, but for their potential.

The Men (Luke 6:14-16)

We do not know a great deal about the men Jesus chose (nothing about some of them), but that in itself is revealing. They were not superstars or platform performers. They continued to serve after Jesus' departure (except Judas Iscariot) without shifting the honor from Jesus to themselves.

None of these men accomplished great things before following Jesus. With the exception of Matthew, none was known beyond a small circle of acquaintances. They did not have educational degrees that would attract attention. The leaders of that day understood that Peter and John were uneducated and untrained men (Acts 4:13).

What made these men so great then? They had been with Jesus (Acts 4:13), but so had many others. These men were special because they were enthusiastic, committed, compassionate, honest, willing to work, and open-minded. Jesus saw their potential and changed their life-directions, while at the same time He allowed for their unique personalities and abilities.

Using our worldly logic we might have chosen quite different men. We would not have chosen an arrogant braggart, two spoiled brats, a con-artist, or revolutionary rebel, would we? But Jesus chose the braggart Peter, who sometimes tried to tell Jesus He was wrong (Matthew 16:22). Peter liked to announce what He would do, but He did not always do it (Matthew 26:33, 69-75). Two spoiled brats—James and John—wanted top billing in the kingdom (Matthew 20:20, 21) and let their tempers get the best of their judgment (Luke 9:51-56); yet Jesus chose them and nicknamed them "Sons of Thunder" (Mark 3:17). Matthew was a tax-collector and would have been considered as a cheat and a scoundrel by many people, but Jesus saw his possibilities. Simon the Zealot was a rebel, but Jesus rescued him. (A "Zealot" was a revolutionary.)

We must consider what happened to these doubtful figures. Arrogant Peter became humble; the marsh-mallow who denied Jesus became a rock (Acts 4, 5). Instead of thinking he had all the answers, he pointed to Jesus in all his sermons. Humbly he followed God's guidance about the admittance of the Gentiles into the church (Acts 10). The tornadoes, James and John, became calm and loving. James was the first apostle to be executed (Acts 12:1, 2), and John wrote an impeccable account of Jesus' life.

We know less about the other apostles, but we can make a few conclusions. Andrew was very personable and often introduced others to Jesus (John 1:40-42). Philip was practical and logical (John 14:8). Nathanael was a man without guile (John 1:47). Thomas needed evidence for belief (John 20:24, 25). Judas managed the money (John 12:4-6). Except for Judas, who committed suicide, and John, who died a natural death, it is thought that all the apostles were executed for their courageous preaching about Jesus.

The Method

How could such men be changed and become great witnesses for the Lord? Because of the way Jesus trained them, and because of their willingness to be changed.

Jesus was not interested in winning the world instantly or in using sensational methods to get a hearing. He was interested in sincere men who would love their fellowmen. He was not interested in short-cut programs to attract the population; He was interested in people who could attract others to Him with their lives and lips. Thus He chose twelve men to be His legacy, to be His delegates, and to win the world.

To be with Him. Jesus called the apostles to fellowship with Him first of all: "And He appointed twelve, that they might be with Him . . ." (Mark 3:14). Jesus was the example, and He wanted them to know Him and imitate Him. He did not want them to just memorize explanations. He not only called them to "come and hear" but also to "come and see." He was a constant "show and tell" for them.

He delighted in spending time with them. He treated them as His interns. Wouldn't it be great if preachers would train young people in this way? They could select mature interns to be with them while they make hospital calls, shut-in calls, and evangelistic calls, while they handle weddings and funerals.

This type of fellowship should not be reserved for just the preacher and a few selected youth. The entire church develops leaders through the power of its fellowship. We need each other. We teach each other, and we learn from each other. When we evangelize someone, it is with the idea that he will be *with us* as well as with God and Christ (1 John 1:3). We must be careful, however, that we do not get people to worship us instead of Christ.

To do for Him. Jesus' call was not just "come and see"; it also included "go and do." At the outset, He let the men know that they were to be fishers of men (Matthew 4:19). He would call them in, but would also send them out (the word "apostle" literally means "sent out"). He did not expect them to be professional students all their lives. They were to graduate and scatter.

Jesus made it clear that it would be costly to follow Him. He refused to let some people stay with Him because they did not count the cost ahead of time (Matthew 8:18-22; Luke 14:25-35).

Is it possible that we are guilty of not letting people know at the outset that becoming a Christian involves both blessings and burdens, favors and functions? We can't have one without the other. Many times we call people to Christ by dangling the many advantages in front of them and do not mention that certain things are expected of them as well. We must show them the many Scriptures that emphasize both sides of God's call:

Blessing	Burden
But you are a chosen race, a royal priesthood, a holy nation, a people for God's own possession	that you may proclaim the excellencies of Him —1 Peter 2:9
. . . who reconciled us to Himself through Christ	and gave us the ministry of reconciliation —2 Corinthians 5:18

Jesus also allowed His apostles to perform when He wasn't with them. In fact, He commanded them to go without Him (Matthew 10). He sent them out to work, much as a mother bird forces the young out of the nest to try their wings. Jesus did not want eternal "nest-sitters."

Jesus was an administrator, but not a snoop or a dictator. He called men with different abilities and personalities, gave them responsibilities, and allowed them the freedom to carry out their responsibilities.

A dictator-leader demands that every person clear every minute action with him before doing anything. He has to put his stamp of approval on every word and action. Sometimes a preacher or a church board can act like a dictator. This is not Jesus' way. He allows us responsible freedom, but not unbounded license.

Just before my present career, I was an air traffic controller journeyman at O'Hare airport. Part of my job was to train new controllers. I guided them, trained them, listened to every word they said on the air, and wrote critiques about their work. When I decided a trainee was ready for a position, I signed a "check out" statement. He needed five such statements from different journeymen before he was left to operate by himself.

What would have happened if I had decided I was going to be the superstar controller and not allow my trainee to become a controller? The work would have stopped when I and other journeymen did.

A leader who wants to be the superstar in the church and not allow anyone else the freedom to develop will stifle Christianity. We must seek to help others grow into leaders. We must put aside our jealousies and selfishness.

For Him to be in them. Jesus didn't stop at association and delegation. He promised that He himself would always be with His apostles. He would send the Spirit who would be their companion and guide (John 14:15-18, 26; 15:26, 27; 16:7-15; Acts 1:8). What strength and hope this promise must have given them! No wonder His legacy had such power and boldness. Neither will Jesus abandon us when we do His work (Matthew 28:19, 20). We are the extension of His legacy today. We can have the same power and boldness through His Spirit (2 Timothy 1:7) though we do not have all the powers the apostles had (2 Corinthians 12:12).

ten

Very Special Characters

Matthew 5—7

The old saying, "You can't judge a book by its cover," is certainly true in many cases. A new movement had begun, but who would have thought it would amount to much?

Its leader, Jesus, did not have an appearance that attracted people or that demanded attention:

> He has no stately form or majesty that we should look upon Him, nor appearance that we should be attracted to Him.—Isaiah 53:2

He was from a poor, humble family that lived in the small town of Nazareth, which had a bad reputation. He was criticized by religious leaders and rejected by His own people. He would not use sensationalism to further His cause, and He refused short-cut opportunities to become ruler of the world.

The group of men that surrounded Him were no prizes, either. They were uneducated, common laborers with calloused, sweaty hands. Some had faces weatherbeaten by the wind of the sea, and they smelled like fish. One was considered dishonest by many; another's political opinions were suspect. And all of them were beset by human frailties.

Yet the new movement that Jesus began and that these men carried on changed the character of the world and continues to do so today. How did they do it? Certainly not because of their "covers"—their great looks or magnetic personalities—but because of their "content."

Jesus was different on the inside. His attitudes and activities were unique—the attitudes and behavior of God. And His personal delegates—the apostles—became transformed through their association with Him. They changed on the inside, which resulted in Christlike (therefore Godlike) lives being lived on the outside. Thus they became engaged in turning the world right side up (Acts 17:6).

The Sermon on the Mount

Shortly after Jesus chose His apostles, He laid the groundwork for the transformation of their characters by preaching what is called the "Sermon on the Mount." He clearly taught them what was expected of them if they were to continue to be His special delegates. He stressed the personal characteristics they would have to develop, their relationship to God, and their relationships to their fellow men.

Let us take a brief glimpse into the character Jesus expected in His followers, His true disciples, members of His family, citizens of the new kingdom. We find the outline of that character in the great address that we all call the Sermon on the Mount.

Blessed are you. The word *blessed* stresses inner joy. God created us to have a certain inner nature; but sin ruins that image, so we do not function as God intended and thus we do not have full joy. But when we choose to turn back to God and develop the right characteristics, our inner natures can be restored and we can experience true joy.

Blessed also means congratulations. Jesus was congratulating those who function as God intended. The word also emphasizes the idea of buoyancy. A person who develops these qualities of life will remain afloat throughout all the storms.

Humility (poor in spirit). The humble person realizes that he needs spiritual help. Jesus was describing a person who is like a beggar—crouching and asking for help. He admits his need for God and also for other people.

No Christian is strong enough to hold together without the Spirit that God gives and without the support of other Christians. The humble person will participate in a contributing fellowship (1 Corinthians 12:12-31; Romans 12; Ephesians 4:15, 16; Hebrews 10:23-25; 1 John 1:3, 4).

Few things can hurt spiritual growth more than the arrogant attitude of independence that cuts us off from both God and others. No man is an island; when he tries to be, he is washed under by tidal waves that result from the earthquakes that sooner or later come into his life.

Sensitive to needs (they that mourn). One who mourns does not wear blinders so he will not see hurts all around him; neither does he become so distracted by his race for success that he does not have the time or inclination to help those who are hurt, wounded, or discouraged. He does not become either tough-skinned or hardhearted.

Neither is he a whining crybaby. He knows how both to rejoice with those who rejoice and to weep with those who weep (Romans 12:15). He is sorry both about his own sins and about the sins of people around him. He will repent and will also lead others to repentance. He does not just weep, but he also acts. He does not just sit around and say "how sad"; he serves with compassion.

Under control (meek). The word *meek* was used of wild stallions after they were tamed. We are not to live wild, out-of-control lives, but we are to be under God's control. The New American Standard Version uses the word *gentle* instead of *meek,* but the meaning is the same.

The word also described an ointment that was used to take the sting out of wounds. The meek one is a person who calms storms rather than creating them. He soothes when people are hurt, rather than reopening the wound and pouring salt on it.

We must not confuse the meek person with a weak person. It takes a great deal of strength not to retaliate when the world digs its spurs into your sides. It takes great control to carry the weight of many burdens of life without bucking or fighting back. And as Jesus said, it is the person who is under control who will win in the final analysis—not the one who bucks and runs wildly.

Hungry and thirsty for the right. Jesus said we should not live on junk food. He wants us to become addicts of God's health food. Christians need to become as enthusiastic about God's food as they are about man's food fads. I know people who will take several vitamin pills each day, will spend much money on "pure" food from health stores, and will subscribe to all sorts of health magazines to know how to better their nutiritional diets. But do you know what is going to happen to their bodies? They are going to die with or without vitamin pills and "pure" food. The body is just temporary.

Our spirits are eternal, yet many are starving. Are we putting God's Word into our minds as diligently as we put food into our stomachs? Are we exercising our spiritual hearts as committedly as we exercise our physical hearts?

When we are truly hungry and thirsty, we do something about it. We don't just sit around and hope that once a week someone will drop some food down our throats. We have such a craving for righteousness that we seek for it and will not be satisfied with just a little taste (Proverbs 2:1-9).

Benevolent (merciful). Mercy is both an inner feeling and an outward function. It is feeling with another person in his situation. It is that inner ache we have when we see another person in need. The need may be spiritual or physical; the merciful person relates to both. And mercy includes doing something about that need.

It is time for church leaders to quit spouting the cliche that we are to be concerned about only spiritual needs. People are not divided into unrelated parts; they are units and act as whole persons. *All* of their needs have always been concerns of God (read Proverbs, Amos, Micah, etc.), and it is time for them to be ours also.

Integrity (pure in heart). Jesus wants us to be the same on the inside as we are on the outside. We are not to have hidden motives behind our actions. He wants no one to have to second guess us. We are always to be the same, no matter whom we are with or where we are. We are not to seek anything for our own advantage only; we are not to be spiritual "politicians." We are to be sincere and pure.

The pure person is genuine; he does not have carefully hidden flaws. His sins are not covered up with cosmetics; the chipped places are not hidden with wax; the rust is not camouflaged by paint.

Jesus does not expect us to be perfect (though He expects progress toward it), but He does expect us to be pure. If we have faults, then we should admit them and seek to change them. We are not to specialize in cover-ups.

Making peace. A person with all the before-mentioned qualities will relate well with others and will be constantly breaking down barriers that separate people. He will not cut others down with his tongue (Matthew 5:22); he will take the initiative to patch up difficulties (Matthew 5:23-26); he will not divorce his wife for his own pleasure (Matthew 5:27-30); he will follow through with his promises (Matthew 5:33-37); he will not retaliate (Matthew 5:38-48); he will not seek for self-glory (Matthew 6:1-18); he will forgive wrongs done to him (Matthew 6:14, 15); he will not worry about himself (Matthew 6:19-34); he will not be too critical of others (Matthew 7:1-6); he will depend upon God (Matthew 7:7-11); he will treat others as he wants to be treated (Matthew 7:12); he will not be detoured to go the way of the crowd (Matthew 7:13-23); and he will not be destroyed by the storms of life (Matthew 7:24-27).

The conduct of the one who makes peace comes directly from his character and is explained in detail in the Sermon on the Mount. However, this type of conduct or life-style is not always welcomed with open arms.

The persecuted. He who seeks to follow Jesus must be ready to be unappreciated. Jesus did not call us to Him just for the blessings and the delights. He warned us that there will be blastings and difficulties. Life with Jesus is not always a "bowl of cherries"; often it is filled with sandpaper rubbing up against us.

But when the persecution is the darkest, our lights can shine the brightest. That is not the time to put lids on our activities (Matthew 5:14-16); it is the time to be more active. When the treatment we are getting is the most rotten, our salt will have its greatest effect (Matthew 5:13).

Jesus was warning the disciples (then and now) that the person who follows in Christ's steps and develops His kind of character will not always be respected in the community. There will always be the Judases around to turn us in, the jealous mobs who want to wipe us out, and the Pilates who know we are right but are more interested in popularity than in being right. But we can expect help from God and from God's people. And we can expect God's blessings now and the final victory later.

Growing Up

Jesus did not expect the apostles to be transformed instantly into the special characters He wanted them to be. He did not expect them to reach spiritual maturity magically. He knew that they would begin as babes and would develop daily, much in the same way they grew physically.

He knew He could not yank them into spiritual adulthood. He was patient with them and allowed them to suffer their growing pains. He knew that was the only way to grow strong spiritual men. Dandelions grow very rapidly, and they disintegrate as rapidly. An oak tree takes many years to grow. It braves the elements and becomes stronger and taller. It does not die when the storms come or when the snow falls. Jesus was concerned that His apostles be oak trees, not dandelions.

He is just as patient with us today. We begin as babes, and we seek daily to be transformed into His image. In spiritual maturity we will have very special characters—after the likeness of Christ.

eleven

A Very Special Kingdom

Matthew 13:1-53; Mark 4:1-34; Luke 8:4-18

In Jerusalem, a man who had been lame thirty-eight years now walked the streets (John 5:1-9); in Nain, a young man who had been en route to his own burial now went about his daily affairs (Luke 7:11-17). In Capernaum, a slave was restored to health (Luke 7:1-10) and a despised woman was given her dignity (Luke 7:36-50); elsewhere in Galilee, a man who had been demon-possessed, blind, and dumb was now as healthy as his neighbors (Matthew 12:22). These were only a few of the many who were helped marvelously by Jesus. "They brought to Him all who were ill . . . and He healed them."

Throngs of people from all over came to hear and see the man who was responsible for these significant happenings. They would put down their tools, close their shops, stop their children's schooling, and even change some of their vocational plans just to get a chance to be in His presence. For this man—the most important man who ever walked on this earth—did more than restore health by His touch. He also restored hearts by His truth.

Yes, Jesus was becoming quite popular. On some occasions, His main problem was managing to position himself so He could be seen and heard by the crowds. So it was one day by the Sea of Galilee. The sloping beach was an ideal place for a huge audience, but there was no platform for the Teacher. The people nearest to Him crowded so close that He could not be seen by those farther away.

Jesus solved the problem by getting into a nearby boat (Matthew 13:1, 2; Mark 4:1). By pushing out a little way from the land He was separated from the crowd and could be seen by most of the people spread out on the beach.

As He looked over the crowd, He saw people from nearby towns and from far-off cities, from all types of families and backgrounds, and with all levels of understanding. He knew it was not time to spout off fancy words or theological philosophies. He was a master teacher who used simple words and everyday illustrations that painted pictures on the listeners' minds. He often taught in parables. The word *parable* comes from the Greek *paraballo,* which literally means "to throw alongside." To make great truths understandable, Jesus would place them alongside familiar things or events of everyday life. Ideas new to the hearers became clear when they were compared with things well known.

On this particular day, sitting in a boat and looking over the crowds, Jesus used a series of parables to teach about a very special kingdom.

Mixed Responses (Parable of the Sower)

Jesus no doubt knew that many of the people in the crowds had heard His teaching over and over, but some of them did not live changed lives as a result. His own hometown folks had rejected His teaching (Luke 4:16-30), and He had recently verbally condemned three cities for their lack of repentance (Matthew 11:20-24). Jesus had gotten the cold shoulder a lot, but He knew He could not evaluate His success by that alone. There were also some faithful disciples (Luke 8:1-3). He would soon be sending out the apostles on their own (Luke 9:1-6). He wanted them to know that they would receive mixed responses to their preaching and teaching. He also wanted the people in the listening throng to see themselves in His parables and to think of their own response.

Jesus compared the communication of God's word with the sowing of seed. The seed may be of fine quality and have the inner capacity of producing a bumper crop, but the seed will not bear fruit unless the soil does its part. Seed without receptive soil will produce nothing; soil without good seed will produce worthless weeds.

In Jesus' day a farmer sowed by reaching into a bag of seed hung from his shoulder, grabbing a handful, and throwing it around over the soil. In order to cover the good soil he scattered some of the seed in places where it would not be productive.

The hardened reception. Some seed would fall "by the wayside" (King James Version) or "beside the road" (New American Standard Version). Probably the "road" was a footpath that separated the fields and was hardened because of much walking upon it. The seed lay exposed on its surface, and birds ate it as soon as the sower was a few steps away. There was no time for it to take root.

Unless the message of Christ can penetrate into the mind of the hearer, there will be no understanding; and without understanding there will be no alteration of life. The pathway hearers are those who are hardened by the busy traffic in their lives. They have been stepped on so often that they will not soften up to change. They have used their hardened surfaces to protect them from being torn up by the pressure of others, and even the word of Christ bounces off of them like pebbles on concrete. It is promptly forgotten, and the devil helps the process of forgetting.

It is not impossible to convert some of these hearers, but it will take more than one exposure to the Word to do it. The storms of life may soften their hardness, as heavy rains soften the pathway, till they can receive the Word. Or the good living and love of Christian friends may act as a plow to break up hard hearts. We must never give up on these people; we know many have finally heeded the word after many years of rejection. But even if some persist in their rejection and never are won, we must not allow this type of response to discourage us in our work or make us think we are failures.

The shallow reception. Some of the seed fell on rocky soil. We should not picture a place filled with huge rocks, but rather an area that had a layer of rock under a few inches of soil. The seed sprouted quickly, and it looked as if a bumper crop were coming. But because of the rocky layer the roots could not go down more than a few inches. The sun grew hotter as the season progressed, and the roots needed to go deeper for moisture. When they couldn't the plant died. This seed began to grow rapidly, but not permanently.

This pictures people who hear the word and "immediately" (Matthew 13:5) jump onto the bandwagon. Their emotional spark has been lit. But the response that is made in the midst of all the attention, pressure, and praise that accompany a mountain-top emotional decision is not the ideal response. The "instant Christian" has no deep-rooted faith; he cannot take it when all the hoopla is over and the real living must begin. When opposition grows hot he begins to wither and soon dies spiritually. All of us know something about "the worry of the world, and the deceitfulness of riches" (Matthew 13:22). Many of us find it hard to keep these from crowding out our devotion to the Lord. But if we are fully determined to give first place to Jesus we can do it. His Word guides us, and His Spirit gives us strength.

The Christian communicator must be careful that he does not design his message or lessons with this type of person in mind, seeking to give an emotional appeal that will elicit an immediate response with no deep roots. We must not cheapen the magnificence of the word by manipulating people emotionally. We must not use the super-salesman approach that leaves the buyer feeling sorry that he bought the product.

We need to take time to get to know the people who are making decisions. I know of a congregation that will not receive a convert into its fellowship without a personal counseling session. Other congregations receive all comers, but take care with the teaching and care of new members. The idea is to break up that rocky layer, if it exists, so faith will grow deep roots and be able to endure every difficulty that can come.

The crowded-out reception. Some seed is choked to death by the weeds that grow up around it. This represents hearers who do not want to clear out everything from their old lives; they do not give enough room for the word to spread and produce its fruit. They are not willing to pull out and discard the weeds that have already taken root in their souls. Christianity looks great to them on Sunday, but on Monday the competition is too strong for the Christian life-style to make any headway.

The productive reception. Some of the seed falls into good soil; it is not perfect soil, but it has the right priorities. It is penetrable; the rocks have been broken up; the weeds have been cleared out. God's word is able to grow and bear fruit in such hearers, for they put the Christian way first and are committed to the word. These are the hearers whose lives are changed by the word.

A Growing Kingdom (Parable of the Mustard Seed)

Jesus stressed that the kingdom of God never sits still; it grows constantly like a mustard seed. It began quietly and in a small way (with a Babe in a manger instead of a great blast of trumpets and the marching of infantries), but it grew rapidly and blossomed into a great power.

When thinking about church growth, some think the church must stay small to enhance the fellowship and closeness. I imagine they have a tough time with the fact that the first church added three thousand to its fellowship in a single day (Acts 2:41). Then others think we must have spectacularly large churches and get carried away with the grandeur of it all. I imagine they have a tough time with the fact that Jesus had only 120 faithful followers after three years of strenuous work (Acts 1:15).

God certainly is interested in the quality of His kingdom as well as the growth in numbers. He is also interested in diversity. He wants all types of humanity to be included (all the birds that find refuge there).

A Transforming Kingdom (Parable of the Leaven)

The kingdom not only grows in size and develops its own people; it also has a good effect on the culture in which it resides. The kingdom changes society as a bit of yeast transforms the dough. The kingdom reaches into every area of life to make it better, slowly and carefully, changing lives and influencing society by the power of changed lives. Is your church—your part of the kingdom—doing its job in your community?

A Priceless Kingdom
(Parables of Treasure and Pearl)

God's kingdom is worth far more than any material wealth, and yet it is free to any that desire it. At the same time, it is costly. We must put the kingdom first on our list of priorities. We must realize the value of the kingdom just as those who found the treasure and the pearl saw their value and sold everything to get them.

A Temporary Mixture
(Parables of Tares and Net)

While the kingdom is the work of God, the devil also does his own planting. In early stages, his plants and those of God look similar; and they stand side by side in the world. Jesus also compared the mixture of the good and the bad with the fish: they swim side by side in the sea. But we are not to be violently plucking up the tares or throwing away the bad fish. The judgment and the separation is God's business. At the end of the age, God will cast out those who do the devil's work and those who are the results of the devil's work.

This doesn't mean we are to neglect the admonishing or disciplining of each other. But it does mean that we are not to be condeming our fellows to Hell. Instead we are to be concerned with sowing the seed, leavening our communities, cultivating the soil, and seeking and finding the proper values. God's kingdom is worth it all—as are the souls who will be saved because of our efforts.

twelve

The Miracle Worker

Matthew 8, 9; Mark 2—6; Luke 5—8

Our three-year-old, Rachel, is the late sleeper at our house, which means she usually doesn't get up until 7:30 a.m. But when she does emerge, she always enters our presence with some sort of announcement—she's tired, she's hungry, she wants to go play, etc. We never know what to expect. Our favorite entrance is when she appears with a wide grin and bubbles out, "Surprise!"

The entrance of God's Son into the ordinary affairs of human life carried with it many unexpected teachings and happenings. And I imagine the favorite surprises from Jesus were the miracles He performed. They were called *signs* because they pointed to something beyond themselves, and *wonders* because they made people wonder.

Why Have Miracles?

We have already discovered that Jesus did not desire to use sensational methods to gain a following, but what else can we call the miracles except sensational? If He did not want to create a sensation, then why did He do signs and wonders?

To establish credentials. Jesus was not the first one to do miracles. During particular times in history, God gave certain persons the power to work signs and wonders—Moses, Joshua, Old Testament prophets, Jesus, the apostles, and New Testament prophets. Each of these persons had a new revelation from God to share with men, and each was sharing his revelation at a time when people had reason to doubt that he was a genuine messenger from God, or when people had a hard time distinguishing truth from falsehood.

Moses was a murderer who had been in exile for forty years. Why should people believe him when he suddenly returned and declared himself their leader? God realized that the people would be reluctant to receive Moses, so He gave Him the ability to work miracles (Exodus 4:1-5). God was, in essence, confirming the credentials of Moses to the people.

God repeated this action many times throughout Jewish history so the people could always be sure who His true spokesmen were:

> Jesus the Nazarene, a man attested to you by God with miracles and wonders and signs which God performed through Him in your midst—Acts 2:22.

> God also bearing witness with them, both by signs and wonders and by various miracles and by gifts of the Holy Spirit according to His own will.—Hebrews 2:4.

Jesus himself observed that His works confirmed His identity (John 9:3, 4; 10:25, 37, 38; 14:11).

To show compassion. Jesus' miracles did more than show that He was God's Son. They also showed something of God's nature. He did not do spectacular miracles that ministered to no one, but miracles that were kind and helpful. Thus the miracles communicated God's compassion for man. It was after Jesus performed many miracles that we read this summary statement:

> And seeing the multitudes, He felt compassion for them, because they were distressed and downcast like sheep without a shepherd.— Matthew 9:36.

Most of Jesus' miracles were beamed toward the hurts of the people of His day. He healed the sick, raised the dead, and cast out demons. He taught the people through these actions that God is a God of love as well as a God of law, a God who cares as well as commands, a God who has sympathy as well as understanding of their problems.

Unexpected Promise (Matthew 9:1-8; Mark 2:1-12; Luke 5:17-26

Jesus had compassion for man's sick body, but He also had compassion for man's sick soul. He did not come just to make everybody physically well; He wanted to make everybody spiritually well. Jesus knew that His motives and messages could be misunderstood if He did nothing more than heal the sick.

On one occasion when a physically paralyzed man was brought to Jesus, Jesus dealt not only with that paralysis but also with the paralysis of his soul: "Take courage, My son, your sins are forgiven" (Matthew 9:2). Jesus was concerned that the man be able to use his legs, but He wanted him also to be able to live his life properly.

The scribes and Pharisees were shocked. Only God can forgive sins. It was blasphemous for a man to claim to do it. Jesus responded, "Which is easier, to say, 'Your sins are forgiven' or to say, 'Rise, and walk'?" For a mere man, it would be easier to say, "Your sins are forgiven," for no one could check the truth of that. You can't put a person into a laboratory and analyze him with a microscope to see whether his sins have been forgiven or not. That fact has to be accepted by faith. But when one says, "Get up and walk," then everyone present can see whether he has power to back up his words or not.

Jesus was demonstrating His power to forgive sins by showing His power to heal the paralytic physically. If He could not have healed the body, His claim to forgive sins would not have been believed. His reputation would have been in jeopardy. We learn from this miracle that we need to accept by faith the promise that God will forgive our sins (Acts 2:38, 39). Many Christians continue to doubt that God can and will forgive the awful things they have done. We need to believe God's power and promise. Let's not be doubtful as were the scribes and Pharisees.

An Unexpected Touch (Matthew 8:2-4; Mark 1:40-44; Luke 5:12-16

In the first century, lepers were outcasts. The Jews were not to touch them, even accidently. To prevent accidental touches, a leper was required to shout "unclean, unclean," if he walked near other people.

On one occasion, a person "full or leprosy" begged Jesus for healing (Luke 5:12). Considering the circumstances, Jesus might be expected to heal him by remote control, if at all. He had healed others without even being close enough to see them (John 4:46-53). Surely in this leper's case He would just speak a word and go on His way.

But Jesus did the startlingly unexpected—He stretched out His hand and touched the man (Luke

5:13). Jesus could heal without touching, but He touched a leper! He was showing that God does not wish to keep His distance from people, even though many of us do.

Many people today have a stigma attached to them for some reason or another. Some are dirty, some are poor, some have been in prison. These people need closeness of fellowship—yes, even some touching—to know that God really cares about them. How can they know God's care if God's representatives on earth try to minister to them by long distance? They may feel little self-worth, may feel like crying, "Unclean, unclean," when they are with "decent" folks. We can teach them God's love and care by talking with them, listening to them, eating with them, and just being seen with them.

An Unexpected Command (Matthew 8:23-27; Mark 4:35-41; Luke 8:22-25)

Jesus and His disciples got into a boat, and Jesus said, "Let us go over to the other side of the lake" (Luke 8:22). It would be a five-mile trip, so Jesus settled down for a nap. That lake (the Sea of Galilee) was an appropriate place for the saying, "If you don't like the weather, wait awhile; it will change." Often the water was whipped by sudden fierce winds from the mountains on the west.

While Jesus slept, one of those sudden storms came up. The wind blew so hard that even the seasoned fishermen among Jesus' disciples were certain that their lives would be lost (Mark 4:38). They had forgotten that Jesus had said, "Let us go over to the other side," and not "Let us go out and drown." They did not yet understand Jesus' power or have full confidence in God's protection.

How could Jesus sleep with such a storm raging all about Him? The same way people today can sleep well even though the world around them seems to be falling apart. People who know that God is in control of the world can go to sleep without being plagued by worry.

Jesus did not have to sit around and wring His hands. He knew the power of the storm was subject to the power of God. When the disciples woke Him, Jesus gave a surprising command. He spoke to the wind and the sea and told them to be still (Mark 4:39). The forces of nature obeyed Him as a trained dog obeys his master.

We learn from this miracle that God is indeed in control of the universe. He is the Lord of all. History is His story. God will not allow circumstances to take over completely. He can make a powerful force become an impotent farce. He has done it to nature, and He has done it to human empires that have threatened to get out of control. We may be at our wits' end when life is raging around us; but God is always there, calm and assured.

An Unexpected Death (Matthew 8:28-34; Mark 5:1-17; Luke 8:26-39)

Soon after the sea was calmed and Jesus and the disciples were ashore, they encountered a wild man who needed to be calmed. He was so berserk that he did not know his name; demons possessed him and spoke with his voice (Luke 8:30).

Demons are the devil's helpers, and they harm whomever they possess. But they are threatened by Jesus and retreat from His presence (Luke 8:28); and rightly so, for they know their final destiny is in the lake of fire. Jesus quickly relieved the man's misery, casting the demons out of him and into some nearby pigs. The pigs were set into a frenzy. They ran wildly down a steep bank and drowned in the sea (Luke 8:31-33).

The people who saw this miracle became quite upset. They observed that the man's sanity was restored, but they were frightened by Jesus' power and concerned about the two thousand pigs that had been destroyed. To them their property was more valuable than a person. They did not want their priorities tampered with, and they wanted Jesus to leave quickly (Mark 5:13-17).

We can learn from this miracle that God considers people more important than a whole hillside of valuable animals. Where are our priorities? Is our fancy furniture more important than our children's activities? Do we spend more money and time on our pets than we do on our friends?

Unexpected Breadth of Compassion
(Matthew 9:18-26; Mark 5:22-43; Luke 8:41-56)

Two miracles were intertwined to give us a beautiful picture of the universal compassion of Jesus (and God).

The synagogue ruler must have had to swallow his pride to beg Jesus for help. He was willing to lose face with his colleagues who hated Jesus and were out to destroy Him. But his daughter was dying, and he risked everything for the chance to have her healed (Luke 8:41).

While Jesus was en route to the house of this man of *high* status in society, a woman with *no* status touched His robe. She had spent all her money trying to find a cure for her hemorrhaging, but had found no help (Mark 5:25, 26). She was just one of many people in the crowd. She shouldn't have been there, because her sickness was the type that made her outcast from society. Everything she touched became unclean (Leviticus 15:25-27). But she was reaching out for her last hope—Jesus. And Jesus fulfilled her hope by healing her. To Him she was vitally important (Mark 5:30, 34).

In the meantime, the ruler's daughter had died. But that didn't trouble Jesus; He simply brought her back to life (Luke 8:49-56).

Sickness is no respecter of persons, and neither is God. He cares for all—those high in society and those not so high.

Summary

We must not just look at Jesus' miracles and be amazed; we must look beyond them to the greatest miracle of all—Jesus himself and what He can do for our lives. God has promised. God has performed. God has shown His compassion for us all. We simply accept His love, believe His promises, and live in His way.

thirteen

The Great Confession

Matthew 16:13-20; Mark 8:27-30; Luke 9:18-21

It had been two and a half years since Jesus had walked alone toward the Jordan to see John the Baptist. Much had happened. He was now a well-known figure in Palestine. The whole populace knew of Him, of His teachings, and of His miracles. Crowds followed Him from place to place, making it difficult for Him ever to rest or to be alone.

After feeding the five thousand, Jesus refused to continue a program of free meals the next day. He offered deep spiritual teaching instead. "As a result of this many of His disciples withdrew, and were not walking with Him any more (John 6:66). The cross was soon to be a reality. Would He have any followers by that time? Would anyone understand who He was? Would anyone be committed enough to Him to carry on His redemptive mission?

Jesus took His disciples away to Caesarea Philippi for a retreat (Matthew 16:13). He used this time for personal prayer (Luke 9:18), and for private conversation with His apostles—perhaps to firm up their convictions about Him. They had long believed that He was the Christ and the Son of God (John 1:41, 45, 49; Matthew 14:33). Were they still holding to that belief when others were turning away?

The Speculation

During one of His conversations with the twelve, Jesus asked an important question: "Who do people say that I am?" (Mark 8:27). Notice he did not ask what people were saying about His actions or about His character or His motives, but about who He was.

During His ministry, His "image" had changed drastically. Once people had said He was Jesus of Nazareth (John 1:45) or the carpenter's son (Matthew 13:55). Now they could tell He was more than that. They connected Him with the Messianic era, but they did not say He was the Messiah himself.

Some said He was John the Baptist. King Herod of Galilee had put John to death, and his guilty conscience made him fear the dead man had returned to life (Mark 6:16). Naturally the king's opinion was repeated by many.

Others said He was Elijah. It was a common belief that Elijah would come as a forerunner to the Messiah (Malachi 4:5, 6). Elijah had been a fiery preacher who had denounced sin, and Jesus' sermons may have been similar to the pople's idea of Elijah's preaching. Indeed He did quite plainly condemn the Pharisees and unbelieving people (Matthew 15:1-14; 11:20-24). But to see Jesus as a forerunner was to miss seeing Him as the Messiah.

Others thought He was Jeremiah. Jeremiah was known as the weeping prophet who lamented over the sins of Jerusalem. Evidently the people could see that Jesus cared for them and was concerned about sin. Jeremiah did not advise rebellion against the oppressive Babylonians, but said the Jews should pray for the welfare of Bablyon (Jeremiah 29:7). Jesus likewise did not spend time condemning Rome. He knew that if Palestine was to change it would have to change from within. Like Jeremiah, He saw the importance of a good heart (Jeremiah 31:33; Matthew 12:34, 35).

Still others did not identify Jesus as a person of the past but as a "personality type" of the past—"one of the prophets" (Luke 9:19). Jesus did not sound like the scribes who were teachers among the Jews. He taught "as one having authority" (Matthew 7:29). So the old prophets had taught. They had their messages from God and gave them plainly.

Yes, many of the people in the massive crowds had come not to see the Son of God, but someone else. When Jesus did not turn out to be what they expected, they withdrew from Him and soon would kill Him. Jesus did not fit their expectations, and He refused to be molded by their pressure into the image they wanted.

Professors in some seminaries today are teaching that Jesus is not divine. They accept the idea that He was a good prophet and a good man, but not the Son of God. However, that teaching today does not change the reality any more than the feelings of the people in Jesus' day did. Jesus is who He is; He cannot be molded into what people want.

Jesus asked what people were saying, but He was more vitally concerned about what His apostles saw in Him. So He asked them a personal question: "But who do you say that I am?" (Matthew 16:15). The emphasis in the Greek construction is on the word *you.* Getting right down to the bottom line, Jesus did not want the opinion of "the man on the street" or the quotes from the "experts." He wanted to know the personal belief of the apostles.

And so it is with us. Our relationship with Jesus does not depend upon our great knowledge of theological positions, but upon our personal belief about Jesus. We can't rest upon what our parents say, what our teachers say—only what we ourselves believe.

The Confession

Peter answered Jesus' question with "Thou art the Christ, the Son of the Living God" (Matthew 16:16). That answer was correct, and so aptly stated that we often ask people to repeat it word for word when they wish to become Christians. We must remember, however, that sincere belief in Jesus is more important than the exact words in which it is stated. In fact, Mark and Luke do not record Peter's words exactly as Matthew does (Mark 8:29; Luke 9:20). In some versions Acts 8:37 records a statement of faith in slightly different form. In our time converts too often are asked to repeat the exact words of Peter without knowing exactly what they mean. *Christ* is from a Greek word meaning *anointed.* In ancient times prophets, priests, and kings were anointed. To say Jesus is the Christ is to say He is the prophet who gives us God's message without fail, He is the priest who obtains forgiveness for us by the sacrifice He offered, and He is the king whom we obey without question. We include some of these truths when we ask a convert to accept Jesus as his Savior and as his Lord. And to say Jesus is the Son of the living God is to say He is divine, He is God as well as man. To state such a faith in one's own words is better than to repeat Peter's words without understanding them.

Peter's response must have been refreshing to Jesus on the heels of all the negative feedback He had received. It must have been encouraging to hear that His apostles did believe in Him and were committed to Him. He knew that, though few in number, they could change the world. Jesus' method of choosing a committed few proved to be effective, for within two years from the time of this confession Christianity embraced more people than the mathematicians could keep up with (Acts 2:41; 4:4; 5:14; 6:7). The "mustard seed" indeed became a tree.

It was not difficult for Peter to declare his faith in the presence of Jesus' friends, but it became tougher when the crowd changed. Less than a year later, when Jesus was put on trial, Peter would not even admit that he knew Jesus (Matthew 26:69-75).

Perhaps the most revealing test of our faith is not what we say on Sunday in worship service, but what we say amidst the unbelievers at work on Monday.

The divine power. A person does not stand up for Jesus against the crowd all by himself. When one truly accepts Jesus as the Son of God, that decision is due to the working of God as well as the person's own mind. Jesus responded to Peter, "Blessed are you . . . because flesh and blood did not reveal this to you, but My Father who is in heaven" (Matthew 16:17). This does not mean that God planted conviction in Peter's mind apart from anything the flesh-and-blood Jesus did. Peter saw Jesus working with divine power; he heard Jesus teaching divine truth. Through what Jesus said and did, God convinced Peter that Jesus was the Christ, the Son of God. We do not see and hear Jesus ourselves, but the inspired record of what He said and did convinces us. When we confess Jesus, it is not the result of mere intellectualism or of guessing the right answer. God convinces us—God working through Jesus and the inspired writers who gave us the record of Jesus.

The careful consideration. Peter's confession (which was in reality the confession of all the apostles) was not a spur-of-the-moment outburst caused by the emotional high of the moment. It was the affirmation of a growing conviction that began with their first encounter with Jesus.

John the Baptist declared that Jesus was the Lamb of God (John 1:29, 36). After only one encounter with Jesus, Andrew told Peter, "We have found the Messiah" (John 1:40, 41). Nathanael confessed, "You are the Son of God; You are the King of Israel" (John 1:49).

A few disciples knew about Jesus' first miracle and believed in Him then (John 2:1-11). When He walked on the water, the apostles affirmed, "You are certainly God's Son" (Matthew 14:33). They had heard Him forgive sins and they knew that no one could do that but God (Matthew 9:2). They had seen Him command nature as only the Creator could do, and they knew He was no ordinary man (Matthew 8:23-27).

These men had evidence to back their conviction, so when the crowds said one thing, they said another. Their conclusion did not flash into their minds when the majority pushed a button. At times they were weak. At times they lacked understanding. At times they almost despaired. Yet they were able to bounce back and become useful vessels for Christ.

The Rock and Foundation

As Peter affirmed Jesus' identity, Jesus reaffirmed the nickname that He had given to Peter in their first encounter (John 1:42; Matthew 16:18). *Petros* in the Greek meant a small stone such as was broken out of a quarry. Even though Peter was a "softie" at times, Jesus knew that he would be a firm, unbreakable stone (Acts 3, 4).

Jesus did not promise to build the church on the person of Peter when He said, "Upon this rock *(petra)*, I will build my church" (Matthew 16:18). Up to this point, He had been speaking to Peter personally (you). But now He switched words and said "this rock." This word was different from the one He used to refer to Peter. *Petra* meant a gigantic rock, the bedrock that provides a solid foundation.

Jesus is the "rock" upon which the church is built (1 Corinthians 3:11). He is referred to elsewhere as the rock that followed Israel in the wilderness (1 Corinthians 10:4). And Peter himself referred to Jesus as the rock *(petra,* 1 Peter 2:8). Peter was a smaller rock, but he was not the only one. He wrote that every Christian is a living stone in the spiritual building that God constructs (1 Peter 2:5).

The Bible writers certainly did not think Peter was an infallible pope. He contradicted Jesus (Matthew 16:22). He lied (Matthew 26:69, 70). He had prejudices hard to overcome (Acts 10). Other apostles sent him on errands (Acts 8:14). Paul once corrected him (Galatians 2:11-16). None of this sounds as if he were infallible or even the main leader of the church. It seems rather that he was a growing apostle.

Peter would be a shaky foundation for the church; but if the church is built on Jesus Christ, nothing can overcome her (Matthew 16:18). For Jesus is eternal. They crucified Him, but they could not keep Him in the grave. All the forces of Hell are only a fizzled firecracker compared to His power, for in His resurrection He destroyed the enemy, death. Built upon Christ and His teachings, the church will never fall or fail (Matthew 7:24-27).

But Peter was given a significant responsibility—the keys of the kingdom (Matthew 16:19). Jesus is the door (John 10:9). The key to open that door is the gospel message. Peter was first in taking this message to the Jews (Acts 2) and then to the Gentiles (Acts 10).

Soon other Christians were using the same keys, the gospel (Acts 8:4). Now each Christian has the same responsibility. We must unlock the door of the kingdom for all who will call upon the name of the Lord (Romans 10:13-17). We are to be faithful to what God has already outlined in Heaven just as the apostles were, binding what He binds and loosing what He looses (Matthew 16:19). Only then will the sons of men become the sons of God.

The Son of God became a son of man in order for the sons of men to become sons of God. And part of that mission lies with us. Are we fulfilling it?

fourteen

Teamwork—A Necessity

Matthew 10:1-42; Mark 6:7-13; Luke 9:1-6

During a busy hour, three hundred fifty airplanes would come in and go out of O'Hare Airport in Chicago when I was a controller there. People used to ask me, "How can one man keep up with it all?" The answer—*one* man doesn't. It takes a team of men working together to move traffic.

It is the same way in the work of Christianity. At the end of each day there are 225,000 more people alive than there were at the beginning of the day, even though thousands have died. One person cannot possibly minister to all the people in the world.

For this reason, God established the church. Christ is the head, while the church members are the body or the team that carries Christ's ministry into all areas of the world. One person cannot do all the saving and serving that the world needs today, so the teamwork of the church family is essential. With these thoughts in mind, we consider Jesus' sending of the twelve apostles, the first "team" assembled and trained to carry out His work.

The Situation

Jesus was nearing the end of the second year of His public ministry. The crowds were massive, and the towns and villages were many; but His time was short. With just a year remaining in His earthly life, there was no possible way He could reach all the hundreds of towns with the message of God.

When He saw the multitudes, He saw them as sheep without a shepherd and felt compassion for them (Matthew 9:36). The needs of the people were many, but the workers were few. He could see the harvest was at hand, so Jesus summoned the twelve to get them ready to go out with the message the world needed to hear. This was not an impulsive decision; Jesus had been carefully planning for such a step.

Jesus carefully selected His co-workers. He knew His own personal ministry would need to be supplemented by a trained group of men who would work side by side with Him and then carry on the ministry when He left. Carefully He taught what was expected of a disciple, and modeled it in His own life.

Jesus did not just issue a call for volunteers to join His group. Instead He choose certain men with potential and willingness and extended the challenge to them individually. Perhaps He spent time with each man separately, pointing out how he could make a unique contribution to the total ministry.

Equipment

The major factor in the equipping of the disciples was their opportunity to observe Jesus as He was working. They watched Him teach, preach, and care for the sick, the downtrodden, and the outcasts. They listened as He communicated with people individually. They heard Him answer tough questions; they marveled as He put complex ideas and issues into simple, everyday language. They noticed that He went off by himself in the early morning to pray. They asked Him to teach them to pray.

After Jesus taught the twelve, both in words and by example, He left them free to work in their individual ways. These men had weaknesses—temper, arrogance, selfish desire for positions of honor, impulsiveness. Some of them were unobtrusive and unspectacular, but Jesus trusted them with a very important task.

From a human standpoint, Jesus' group would seem highly unlikely to do great things. Yet Jesus sent them out as His ambassadors. The men knew they were not going out on independent missions of their own. They knew Jesus was to be their guide and leader, and they knew they had specific responsibilities to fulfill. They did not go out to "do their own thing."

The twelve went out by twos. Each one felt not only a responsibility to Christ, but also a responsibility to his partner. Each one sought to strengthen and help his partner's ministry and witness. They did not go out as competitors, but as companions and co-workers.

Jesus impressed upon these men their purpose and responsibility, but He also supplied them with power (Matthew 10:1). He did not withhold His secrets from them for fear they might become as popular as He. He gave them the ability to do signs and wonders just as He had been doing.

The apostles did not accomplish miracles by their own effort. The power was *given* to them. It was God's own power that Jesus shared. In this way, the twelve were certified as inspired messengers of God. The listening people could know that the message was authentic, a message from God (Acts 14:3; Hebrews 2:4).

When enlisting workers in the church, we should learn from Jesus' methods. Instead of just issuing general calls for volunteers, we should be on the alert for persons with special interests and abilities who can do specific jobs. Then we should extend the challenge of each job to those best suited to do it.

All of us who are in positions of leadership need to think about our leading. Often we criticize people of the church because they are not involved, and we bemoan the fact that Christians today are not committed. But how often do we really get down to specifics and point out in detail what needs to be done in the local situation? And then comes the really big question— how often do we *equip* the people to do what is needed? When we find someone willing to work, usually we just smile, pat him on the back, and say "go to it" without giving an ounce of direction or preparation to do the job.

Many preachers and other leaders in the church do their work in isolation. They visit the hospital patients alone; they attend special meetings alone; they make evangelistic calls alone; they prepare for weddings and funerals alone—and then they complain that they have to "do it all." Why not find one or two young men in the congregation who would be interested in accompanying the leaders as they go about their work? This would encourage young men to go into the ministry as well as give them much practical experience.

Church leaders are to equip others to serve (Ephesians 4:11-16). They should be in a continuous process of multiplying themselves through the work of others on the team. No church program is a success if only a few do the work. Jesus' ministry is greatly hampered when the preacher or the elder tries to "do it all." It was too big a job for Jesus, and it is too big a job for one person today.

The Support

The twelve who were sent out by Jesus were not to be independent of Him; neither were they to be independent of human supporters (Mark 6:8-11). They were not to supply their own needs. They were not to fill their own knapsacks, their own money bags, or even their own suitcases. They were to learn to depend upon others.

The people among whom the twelve ministered were to support them financially. This is a consistent Bible teaching. In the Old Testament we see that the priests were materially supported by the people they ministered to. Jesus allowed people to support Him financially (Luke 8:1-3). The Lord himself commanded that those who proclaim the gospel should get their living from the gospel (1 Corinthians 9:14).

Some use Paul's example of making tents as an excuse for not paying preachers (Acts 18:1-3). But a closer study of Paul's practices will not support that position. Paul's tentmaking in Corinth was a very temporary arrangement. He had come into the city alone, while the rest of the team was still in Macedonia. A person who traveled alone knew better than to carry much money. He might be robbed on the highway. So Paul made tents to finance his stay in Corinth. His tentmaking hindered his preaching and teaching activities. He had only one day free to do God's work (Acts 18:4). But when the rest of the team arrived, Paul quit making tents and devoted himself completely to the ministry of the word (Acts 18:5).

Why the change in activity? Probably because the team had brought the money that was needed to finance their work. Although Paul did not receive a salary from the Corinthian congregation, he did receive money from other churches so that he could give his full attention to the gospel proclamation (2 Corinthians 11:7, 8). While Paul was in Thessalonica he worked; but not because he needed the income. He wanted to be an example to some of the church members who were lazy (2 Thessalonians 3:7-12). The church at Philippi sent him money more than once while he was in Thessalonica (Philippians 4:15, 16). He was there only three weeks (Acts 17:1-10), so he did not need the money he made by tentmaking.

It is God's plan that those who serve spiritually should be taken care of physically by those who receive spiritual help (Romans 15:27). "If we sowed spiritual things in you, is it too much if we should reap material things from you?" (1 Corinthians 9:11). Such a plan should not seem unusual or unfair to us. We expect to pay the doctor, the pilot, the printer, the policeman, the teacher, the publisher, the ball player, the pharamacist, and others for the services they render to us. Why should we hesitate to provide for the needs of a preacher?

Since God intends for those who preach the gospel to have their living for their work, we can be sure God takes seriously our willingness or unwillingness to support these workers. He will not take lightly our complaints about supporting these while we give magnificent support to workers in other walks of life.

At the close of His instructions to His disciples, Jesus remarked that God was taking notice of the people who would materially care for them:

He who receives a prophet in the name of a prophet shall receive a prophet's reward; and he who receives a righteous man in the name of a righteous man shall receive a righteous man's reward. And whoever in the name of a disciple gives to one of these little ones even a cup of cold water to drink, truly I say to you he shall not lose his reward.

—Matthew 10:41, 42.

God will reward the smallest material benefit we give to His workers. What a tremendous investment!

It is unkind to expect people to use their income-making time to minister to others and not be paid for it. In our highly industrial and complex society, it is particularly important to have persons free to minister to people's needs. It is not feasible for a foreman to release a worker from the assembly line several times a week to help someone who has a need—a sickness, a death, an emotional problem. God's plan makes special servants available to meet these needs.

Though Jesus sent the twelve without resources of their own, He assured them that they would be well taken care of. But He also made it clear that they were not to manipulate others in order to receive the best material things. They were not to move from house to house in an attempt to get the best accommodations. They were not to keep looking for the best deal—best bed, best food, private rooms, etc. They were to be content to stay in the place that was first made available to them (Mark 6:10).

There is something wrong with motives and attitudes when "servants of God" demand only the best of first-class service. Do they have to stay in the best hotel or have a private room and bath when staying in a home? No man of God should be above staying in the humblest surroundings. God's workers are not to be grabbing for everything material they can get.

On the other hand, God's people are not to be stingy when it comes to sharing with those special workers. It is a tragedy when the church takes advantage of its minister's humility and expects him to live in a hovel while other Christians have much better homes.

The church is a family; she is a team. Each one in the family or team should be looking out for the welfare of other members in the family. The family or team should be a harmonious, loving fellowship. The relationship should be one of sharing, not one of management and labor.

Jesus is in Heaven now. His ministry on earth cannot continue without the teamwork of the church. Jesus can be everywhere only as His people are everywhere. He lives in us to minister through us. Are you doing your part? And are you multiplying your own ministry through others?

fifteen

One of a Kind

Matthew 17:1-8; Mark 9:2-8; Luke 9:28-36

Mountaintops and Valleys

It was an exciting summer; it was like one continuous mountaintop experience. Our son, Randy, was on the local Little League all-star team. They won all the local games in the single-elimination tournaments and became the Missouri state champs. They won the next games and became the champions of ten states. The whole family went to LeMars, Iowa, to cheer the team on in the last tournament before the World Series.

The team made it to the finals. Just one more game and they would go to the World Series. We were ready and felt confident; I had even reserved rooms for us in Williamsport, Pennsylvania, where the World Series would be held. But our team lost. Such a disappointment! The boys, the coaches, and the parents were all crying.

It was tough to realize we had lost when we were so ready to win. We were all dazed, but eventually disbelief was replaced by reality.

It was tough to accept the actuality of the defeat; but if someone had said in advance that the loss was inevitable, that would have been even harder to accept. None of us would have believed it, for we had a really good team.

Neither was it easy for the apostles to accept what Jesus told them immediately after they had confessed that He was the Messiah (Luke 9:20). To admit that Jesus was the Christ was to acknowledge that He was the anointed King whom the Jews had been expecting for generations. The King had finally come! He would take the government away from Rome, put it on His shoulders, and increase it (Isaiah 9:6, 7). The Jews could at last be free!

These twelve men felt that they had picked the World Series Winner and that they would be right there with Him when He was crowned. They were on a continuous mountaintop experience with Jesus. But then Jesus lowered the boom.

He told the apostles that He would go to Jerusalem to suffer and be killed (Matthew 16:21; Mark 8:31; Luke 9:22). He added that he would rise from the dead, but the men evidently did not let that sink in. All they heard was Jesus telling them that defeat was ahead; they did not want to accept it. Peter said, "God forbid it, Lord! This shall never happen to you" (Matthew 16:22).

But in a few months it did happen. The twelve apostles went from the mountaintop to the deepest valley of the shadow of death. They watched their leader nailed to a cross between two crooks; they watched Him die.

As the time of Jesus' death drew nearer, God knew the disciples would need some added reassurance that Jesus was really God's Son. His terrible death could make them think they had chosen the wrong person to follow.

We must realize that the Jews at this time thought that when the Messiah appeared He would never die. Not long after this incident, the people criticized

Jesus' prediction about death with these words: "We have heard out of the Law that the Christ is to remain forever" (John 12:34).

The Unique Change

The awful announcement about Jesus' death was buffered by the glorious experience of the transfiguration. This event was God's way of reassuring the apostles that Jesus was truly God's Son (even though subsequent events would cause them to doubt). God wanted them to know that His apparent abandonment on the cross did not mean that Jesus was an imposter.

Before they were to enter the valley of defeat and disappointment, Jesus led three of His apostles up a hill (Luke 9:28). While He was praying, His appearance miraculously changed (Luke 9:29). The veil of Jesus' humanity was pulled back; with their own eyes Peter, John, and James saw His divinity.

The change is recorded in the verb *metamorphao*, from which we get our word *metamorphosis*. It means to change into another form. The familiar human figure of Jesus changed temporarily into a glorious Heavenly form before their very eyes.

In that temporary change, even Jesus' outer clothing appeared different: "His clothing became white and gleaming" (Luke 9:29). The color white symbolized righteousness (Isaiah 1:18), but Jesus' righteousness was far beyond what any human could produce. "His garments became radiant and exceedingly white, as no launderer on earth can whiten them" (Mark 9:3). It was a whitening from the inside out. Truly God was in Christ.

Although God does not transfigure us as He did Jesus, He does let us know that the tough times we face do not mean we are not His children. God never promised us a rose garden without thorns. Tough times do come to us; we have to bear our own crosses.

But through these experiences we mature and become more like Christ. God does not instantly transfigure us, but He does gradually transform us (2 Peter 1:3-8).

When we are born again, our inner characters change (Ephesians 4:23, 24). That change is to continue. Paul said our minds are to go through a metamorphosis (Romans 12:2), and it is to be a daily transformation. Into what form are we changing? Into the very image of Jesus! (2 Corinthians 3:18).

The story has been told about two caterpillars who were in cocoons. They were observing the beauty of a spring day when a graceful butterfly flew by. One caterpillar turned to the other and said, "You'll never catch me in one of those contraptions." He did not realize that he had come into existence in order to change into one of those butterflies. How sad that he was content to remain in the stagnant stage of the cocoon! It is even sadder when Christians fail to realize that they are called to be transformed into a new existence, to become like Christ.

One day we shall go through the final stage of our metamorphosis: "We know that when He appears, we shall be like Him, for we shall see Him as He is" (1 John 3:2, New International Version). But we are not just to sit around and wait for it; we are to be progressing daily toward being like Him.

The Unique Meeting

The disciples not only saw Jesus change, they also saw two superstars of the past. "And behold, two men were talking with Him; and they were Moses and Elijah" (Luke 9:30). Moses was the lawgiver, and Elijah was representing the prophets. Both of them had anticipated the promised Messiah. They now knew in what specific person God would manifest himself (1 Peter 1:10, 11).

They were discussing Jesus' departure (Luke 9:31). The word *departure* is the Greek word for *exodus.* As Moses had experienced the exodus from Egypt, Jesus would experience the exodus from earth—His death; and in that exodus He would be dying for all men. He would be leading all mankind out of the slavery of sin into the eternal promised land.

It is interesting to note that Moses and Elijah were not dead; they were very much alive. Jesus did not bring them back from the dead. Many Jews believed that once a person died, he remained dead; but Jesus corrected that thinking: "But regarding the resurrection of the dead, have you not read that which was spoken to you by God, saying, "I am the God of Abraham, and the God of Isaac, and the God of Jacob? God is not the God of the dead but of the living" (Matthew 22:31, 32).

To die in faith is to be alive with God. We do not know all the details about life after death, but we do know that to be absent from the body is to be present with the Lord (2 Corinthians 5:8). Jesus said that those who believe in Him have passed out of death unto life (John 5:24), and those who live and believe in Him shall never die (John 11:26).

Death is to the believer what birth is to a baby. It is God's way of transferring us from one environment into another. There is no need for Christians to live as if they were attending a continuous funeral. We should be living victorious and joyful lives, even in the face of death.

The Immature Choice

The disciples were so overcome by seeing these great men of the past that they attempted to give them equal billing with Jesus. "Peter said to Jesus, 'Master, it is good for us to be here; and let us make three tabernacles: one for You, and one for Moses, and one for Elijah'—not realizing what he was saying" (Luke 9:33).

The disciples took their eyes off Jesus and became overly impressed with God's human servants. They wanted to elevate them to Jesus' level. They often were overly concerned with human greatness (Matthew 18:1; 20:20-28; Luke 22:24). In their immaturity, they likened Jesus to the great men of the past. But Jesus was not in competition with others: He is one of a kind!

The Old Testament tabernacle was a man-made dwelling place for God, but Jesus was superior to that. He was God's God-made dwelling place. Moses and Elijah were God's spokesmen, but Jesus himself was God.

There have been and still are many great people in God's kingdom, but we must never let our admiration of them overshadow our love and faithfulness to Jesus. Jesus is the one who is the bread for the hungry, the water for the thirsty, the healing for the sick, the way for the lost, the life for the dead, the truth for those who err, the door for those who want in, the shepherd for the sheep, and the Savior for all men.

We must be cautious about becoming dazzled by the spectacular. We must not allow our attention to be detoured from Jesus Christ. It is easy to let lesser things become our priorities if we are not constantly on the alert. We must not allow a building program, a great increase in attendance, a great evangelistic method, a powerful human leader, or an attractive project become more important to us than Jesus.

Perhaps you are saying, "Oh, that couldn't happen to me." But if Jesus' disciples could make that mistake after being with Him in person daily for two and a half years, it could also happen to us. We crowd Jesus out when we don't spend time alone with Him in prayer. We crowd Him out when we don't take time to read about His life and teachings. We show where our priorities lie when we don't turn every area of our lives over to Him.

When Peter made the mistakes of equating Jesus with Moses and Elijah, God caused a bright cloud to appear and startle the disciples. Then God declared, "This is my Son, My chosen One: listen to Him"—and only Jesus was seen (Luke 9:34-36). God was restating the confession they had recently made about Jesus (Luke 9:20). But to see Jesus and hear God's declaration about Him were not enough; they were also to listen to Him!

Perhaps we should all go up to the mountain of transfiguration and let God blot out all the distractions that threaten to turn us away from Jesus. Perhaps we should let Him remind us to listen and obey. Only as we look to Jesus can we be constantly changing and becoming more like Him. Only as we look to Him can we become mirrors that reflect His life-style down in the valleys of everyday life.

> Turn your eyes upon Jesus,
>   Look full in His wonderful face,
> And the things of earth will grow strangely dim
>   In the light of His glory and grace.

sixteen

The Costly Commitment

Matthew 8:19-22; Luke 9:57-62

I have not yet met a person who plants rose bushes
for the thorns they produce, not a woman who wants a
baby because of the labor pains, nor a person who
submits to surgery just to feel the knife, nor a person
who takes castor oil for the taste, nor a person who
answers the telephone at 3 a.m. just to be getting up.

Yet at times all of us are willing to accept the thorns,
the unpleasant sensations, and the inconvenient experiences because of goals we wish to attain. Our
forefathers endured much to find a comfortable life in
a free country; and no sooner had they found it than
some of them pulled up stakes again, loaded their be-
longings into covered wagons, and journeyed over
wilderness and desert to carve out for themselves a
new life in the wide-open spaces. Man throughout history has consistently entered into tension-filled and
distasteful experiences in order to reach his goals. It is
thus that great things are accomplished.

A person with no goals will find life meaningless. A
person with too many goals will find life confusing. A

person with goals that are too high will find life frustrating. But a person with attainable goals that serve both God and others will find the abundant life that God intends for each person to have.

God created us with His own basic nature within us. That nature is unselfish, other-oriented; so it is not surprising that psychologists tell us today that we will remain emotional adolescents unless we find a goal that is unselfish and unless we enter into activities that are of service to others. Only in helpfulness do we find our true selves and travel down the road to psychological maturity. One significant researcher goes further and says that most of the people in our mental institutions are not irresponsible because they are mentally ill, but are mentally ill because they have not been responsible in life. They have not developed unselfish goals or lived for others.

Jesus pointed out this same truth in these words from Luke 9:23, 24:

If anyone wishes to come after Me, let him deny himself, and take up his cross daily, and follow Me. For whoever wishes to save his life shall lose it, but whoever loses his life for My sake, he is the one who will save it.

It is easy to live for self, and in that way to lose the self we are living for. For that reason Jesus knew better than to accept the commitments of all those who desired to be on His bandwagon. He knew that some wanted to follow Him for the excitement or for the benefits they would receive rather than for a life of lowly service to others. Jesus did not turn away people from being His followers unless they were turned away by the requirement of complete, unselfish commitment.

Not always would Jesus be the center of enthusiastic followers. Soon He would be executed. He knew that life would be extremely tough for His disciples then. He would need followers whose commitment was complete. He would need followers whose eyes were wide open to the problems they would have to face—but even His closest followers insisted on shutting their eyes to those problems (Matthew 16:21, 22). He did not want men who were even less fully committed, men who were swept away by His sensational miracles, men who would make rash promises that they were not willing to carry out.

The Rash Commitment

As Jesus was going along the road, someone said to Him, "I will follow You wherever You go." Isn't that the type of surrender Jesus wants from all of us? Yes and no. Yes, He wants us to surrender ourselves. No, He does not want us to do so blindly, without thinking of the consequences. The person who said that to Jesus did not know that Jesus was headed for Calvary, that He was going to receive a cross before a crown.

Jesus proceeded to make this person partly aware of what commitment to Him really meant: "The foxes have holes, and the birds of the air have nests, but the Son of Man has nowhere to lay His head" (Luke 9:58).

Jesus wanted the would-be follower to understand that possessions and riches do not come automatically when one becomes His disciple. Real commitment involves counting the cost, not the cash. It calls for denial of self, not just the delights of success. One who wants to be committed to Jesus must be willing to give up all he has instead of grabbing for all he can get (Luke 14:33; Matthew 19:21). Jesus was saying, "I have produced miracles; but if you follow me, don't expect me to produce material things for you."

Jesus was also emphasizing the danger that lies in true commitment. The holes for the foxes and the nests for the birds provided secure hiding places for them to escape from their enemies, but Jesus had no place to hide. One who is committed to Jesus will have to face danger and persecution as Jesus did. The people in Jesus' hometown tried to kill him (Luke 4:29). He was not safe in Judea (John 5:18), in Galilee (Luke 6:11), in Gadara (Matthew 8:34), or in Samaria (Luke 9:53). Jesus' opponents were always after Him.

The Christian who is truly committed to Jesus will not escape criticism, mockery, snubs, and outright persecution. The Christian who stands up in the crowds will get shot down by the critics. By the end of the first century, the property of Christians was confiscated, and many were executed by methods that surpassed even Hitler's methods of killing the Jews. Many Christians were dipped in tar, attached to posts, and then lit like torches to provide illumination for the sports arena. Others were wrapped in fresh animal skins and placed in the arena where starving dogs and wild animals were let loose upon them.

Persecution of Christians in many parts of the world today does not come in such violent forms. We are more familiar with the subtle persecution of our egos. A Christian may lose his job if he does not go along with dishonest ethics. He may acquire the name of "Holy Joe" if he does not curse or listen to dirty jokes. He may be called "chicken" if he does not experiment with drugs or illicit sex. While the methods of persecution have changed, the challenge still remains for the Christian.

But we can find refuge in Christian homes and in the church. The encouragement and support of the family of God is the sustaining force that allows us to go back into the wilderness where we have no protection. No matter what the external circumstances, the Christian knows he will be victorious over all his enemies in the final analysis. To be in Jesus is to have a "hole" and "nest," but the cost factor is not erased.

The Reserved Commitment

Jesus issued an invitation to another (Luke 9:59). This one had some reservations: "Permit me first to go and bury my father." While the first person was too ready, this person was too reserved. Jesus was already going along the road (Luke 9:57), but this man wanted to wait awhile. His life was too crowded with other responsibilities: he did not feel free to go with Jesus. He could not let go of the "worries of the world."

From our standpoint, the request of this man does not seem unreasonable at all. Why couldn't Jesus wait for a funeral? The custom was to bury a person on the same day he died. Couldn't Jesus wait a few hours? Or couldn't He go on His way and let this follower catch up the next day?

Probably the issue was not so simple. Many students suppose the father was not dead, but only old and infirm. His son felt a responsibility to take care of him till his death, and so he wanted to postpone following Jesus for an indefinite time, not just a few hours.

Whether that was the case or not, the man was giving second place to Jesus. His family and social obligations came first. How many people today want to be Christians, but give first place to some other plans? Then if they have any time or energy left over, they will invest it in Jesus' cause. "Maybe someday I'll follow you, Jesus." How many people want to follow Jesus on their own terms and in their own time? But Jesus is the one who writes the contract!

Jesus answered this man with a challenge that emphasized kingdom responsibilities: "Allow the dead to bury their own dead; but as for you, go and proclaim everywhere the Kingdom of God" (Luke 9:60). Those who are not followers of Jesus are dead spiritually, but there are some responsibilities that they can carry out as well as anyone can. If a Christian spends all his time and energy looking after the responsibilities that anyone can manage, he will neglect the vital services that only a disciple of Jesus can do. This does not mean that we are not to be involved in any social or community or family affairs. Christians are to be the light and salt in their communities. They are responsible for their families. But they must put Jesus first! (Matthew 10:37).

Jesus knows all people, and deals with each one individually. When one wanted to bury his father before following the Lord, probably Jesus knew this was one who had a tendency to procrastinate. He needed to hear Christ's words of urgency.

Another man expressed similar reluctance: "I will follow You, Lord; but first permit me to say good-bye to those at home" (Luke 9:61). Jesus knew what would happen if this particular man returned home. Perhaps he was part of a family that would not give its consent for this man to follow an itinerant preacher. Jesus sensed that this young man was too tied to his family to be able to make a firm commitment to Him.

Jesus responded, "No one, after putting his hand to the plow and looking back, is fit for the kingdom of God" (Luke 9:62). Any farmer knows that plowing a straight furrow requires selecting a spot ahead at the end of the field and aiming toward it. To look back would produce a crooked furrow. It is the same situation in the kingdom. We must select the proper goal and work toward it, not allowing things of the world to distract us.

We must be neither rash nor too reserved in our commitment to Jesus. We must be willing to lose our lives for Him. Our hearts and heads must be aiming toward the same goal, and we must be ready to bear the crosses as well as reap the blessings.

seventeen

The Lost Ones

Luke 15

Light is to penetrate darkness. Salt is to flavor food.
Yeast is to be put into dough. A physician is to be in
the presence of the sick. And the Savior came to associate with sinners and to save them.

Jesus came to be involved in people's lives; He did
not come to remain aloof from the pains and problems
of mankind. He confounded the accusers of a woman
who had been caught in the act of adultery, went to
the home of a despised tax collector, allowed a sinful
woman to wash His feet, and dared to cleanse an outcast leper.

The traditionally righteous Jews were appalled by
His actions; "This man receives sinners and eats with
them" (Luke 15:2). To share a meal with someone was
taken to mean that you accepted that person—at least
the Pharisees interpreted it that way in the case of
Jesus. One of them once invited Jesus to dinner; but
to show that it did not mean full acceptance he neglected the common courtesy of water for the feet and
oil for the head (Luke 7:36-48).

To us, the idea of eating with sinners does not sound serious; but to the Pharisees *sinner* was a very degrading designation. Today we refer to sinners in a general way, and most of us include ourselves in that category. At least we call ourselves sinners saved by grace. But the Pharisees held themselves proudly aloof from those they called sinners. One rabbi said sinners should be quartered on the Day of Atonement by tying them to four different horses and making the horses run. A man should not allow his daughter to marry a sinner; a good person would not be a guest in the home of a sinner and certainly would not invite such a person to his home. No business was to be done with a sinner; some Pharisees would not even talk with one.

Thus the religious puritans of the day were cut to the core by Jesus' association with "defiled people." That was no way for a Jewish teacher to act! They had the same attitude that we might have if we saw our elders or preacher socializing with a bartender or a drug pusher.

No doubt Jesus' associations hurt His reputation with others besides the Pharisees, for many people did not understand that He could associate with sinners without participating in their sins. Yet Jesus did not retreat. He had come to show what God was like, and He could not do so if He acted the way the Pharisees wanted Him to act.

But Jesus did try to explain why He associated with sinners. He told three parables that are a great encouragement to the lost and clearly protest against the idea and practice of giving the gospel to good people only. All three parables have two things in common: something is lost, and something is found. But there's one thing that is not the same in all three. Not *everyone* is happy when the lost is found in the last parable.

The Lost Sheep

One sheep of the flock was lost. But it was only a sheep—why get upset? The feeling of that shepherd may be compared to the way we would feel if our Cougar, Mustang, Colt, or Pinto were lost—a four-wheeled animal instead of a four-legged one.

It would be easy for a sheep to wander off in search of food and lose track of his fellow sheep. The shepherd was very much concerned. Even though he had a hundred sheep, he knew them all by name and was startled and grieved when one was missing. It seems to me that if you have seen one sheep you have seen them all; but my wife's brother raises sheep, and no matter how many he has, he knows each one by name. He knows their unique characteristics, and even their registration numbers.

The shepherd looked for the sheep until he found it. It was not just a token search or a quick look through the bushes. It was a total, concentrated search. The shepherd was willing to go anywhere. No place was too dirty, too dingy, or too humiliating for that shepherd to be seen there looking for the lost one. He cared that much.

Where are we willing to go to look for the lost of this world? Or do we expect them to search us out? Do we ever leave the ninety-nine who are safe in the fold? Do we go out into the dark wilderness to find the lost? Do we really go *anywhere*? Or do we pick only a few places to go? Are we willing to go to the dirty, dingy, degrading places to find those who live there? Or would we rather sit on our comfortable pews in our immaculate and luxurious church buildings and hope the lost find God?

A sheep does not take the initiative to find his way out of the wilderness; he simply wanders and waits, hoping someone will help him out of his misery. He needs a guide to the sheltering fold.

People are much like sheep. "All of us like sheep have gone astray, each of us has turned to his own way" (Isaiah 53:6). People do not get lost on purpose. Most of them simply wander away from goodness and safety, too preoccupied with their own little worlds even to notice what they are doing. They wander aimlessly until one day they realize that they are lost. They want to go back, but they don't know how. They need someone who cares enough to find them and show them the way.

When the shepherd found the lost sheep, he had a party and invited his friends to rejoice with him. And Jesus said, "I tell you that in the same way, there will be more joy in heaven over one sinner who repents, than over ninety-nine righteous persons who need no repentance" (Luke 15:7). Jesus was not saying that those who are righteous do not give joy to God. Surely the Father delights in His faithful family members. But there is a special happiness when one is rescued from danger, and the degree of joy is related to the concern and the effort in the search. Any parent who has ever temporarily lost a child understands the feeling. When the child is found, there is more joy *at the time of the finding* because of the worry and concern that were experienced in the search.

The Lost Coin

In the parable of the lost coin, the item that is lost is only one of ten. Why such a big deal about it? Many scholars have suggested that the ten coins may have been the woman's dowry, and therefore may have had great sentimental and symbolic meaning. The marriage might even be in jeopardy if the dowry was not intact. All the neighbor women would have understood the misery of this woman who had lost the one coin, and would have shared her joy when she found it.

Even without any sentimental value, however, the lost coin was no trifle. The *drachma* was nearly the same as the Roman *denarius,* which appears in Matthew 20:2 as a day's pay for a laboring man. That amount would be significant in any culture. To many workers today it would be as much as fifty or seventy-five dollars. I imagine most of us would search frantically if we lost that much.

We can see the woman, worried and upset, earnestly searching for the money, hoping to find it before her husband got home. She lit a lamp to search the shadowed corners; she swept the dirt floor diligently. (A woman of today would look under the sofa cushions and in the bureau drawers.) And when the coin was found, she called in her friends and neighbors to share in her great joy.

The Lost Son

The Pharisees' reaction is not recorded. We cannot tell whether they got the point of those two parables or not. But Jesus hit closer to home when He talked about a lost person, a sinner.

A young son wanted to go his own way and do his own thing. He would be entitled to a part of his father's estate when his father died, but he couldn't wait; he wanted everything now! He left home and wasted or squandered his money. The Greek word literally means he scattered it. It was as if he were carelessly throwing money to the wind. He spent the money in loose living, or riotous living, as the King James Version has it. His life-style was abandoned, dissolute. The Greeks used the same word of the hopelessly sick. This young man was living a sick kind of life; he was destroying himself with wild, disorderly, and dissipated living. See the same word used in Ephesians 5:18; Titus 1:6; 1 Peter 4:4. The New American Standard Version translates it dissipation; the King James

Version has excess or riot. In that kind of living the young man lost all of his money and all of his so-called friends at the same time.

All too soon the young man found himself alone, broke, friendless, and caring for hogs. What a miserable sight he must have been! He was no doubt dirty, unkempt, and stinking. He had no money for soap. A Jew could not get much lower than being a caretaker of pigs, which were considered to be unclean and detestable animals. He really hit bottom when he began wishing to have some of the pigs' food to eat. The pods were scarcely fit for human consumption, but he was desperately hungry. It would be much the same if someone today would be reduced to eating dog food to stay alive, or reduced to digging garbage out of the trash cans.

Fortunately the young man realized that he did not have to stay in that style of life. He could go back home and have food and shelter. He realized what he had done and took responsibility for it. He became man enough to stop demanding his own way. He had lived only for himself, but now he was willing to be a servant and live for others. He realized that those who lived for others were much better off than those who lived selfishly. Thus he repented of his sinfulness, expressed his regrets to his father, and offered himself as a servant.

The father declared a holiday and staged a big barbecue with all the merriment that accompanies a festive occasion. He was so happy to have his son back that he wanted to share his joy with others.

How often do we express such joy when a sinner comes to Jesus? Are we really happy when a baptismal service extends the morning worship another fifteen minutes and we can see the line at our favorite restaurant getting longer and longer? How many times after a baptism do we scatter so quickly that the new Christian comes up out of the water, dries off, and faces an empty auditorium? Where is the party atmosphere? Is Heaven the only place where there is rejoicing when a lost one is found?

In these parables Jesus is pointing out that a lost person is a valuable person. Jesus spent time with sinners for the same reason the shepherd looked for his lost sheep and the woman looked for her lost coin.

How about us? Are people as important to us as our pets? Is a person as important to us as money? Or are we like the elder brother, wanting to isolate ourselves from the lost and not being joyful when one comes to the Lord? Do we balk or sulk because he seems to be getting more attention than we, the faithful standbys, are getting? That was the problem of the Pharisees and scribes.

Jesus also was saying that God is like the waiting father; He is watching eagerly and with compassion for the lost ones to return to Him. He allows men to make their own decisions, but He is heartbroken when they turn to go their own mistaken way. He watches anxiously; He continually looks toward the horizon, hoping lost men will be returning. Those who are bankrupt materially and spiritually can come home to God. He is waiting with open arms. And when we do return, God's joy is unspeakable!

THE FATHER IS WAITING FOR YOU.

eighteen

Jesus and Your Checkbook

Luke 16:1-15, 19-31

An old story tells of a man who tied his money belt full of gold around his waist before he jumped overboard from a sinking ship. Later the divers found him at the bottom of the sea with his weighty gold still in the money belt around his waist. His gold owned him and caused his destruction.

There are many in our world today who are just like this man. They think they own their houses, their cars, their land, or their businesses; but in reality, their possessions own them. Their possessions determine how these people spend their time, what they worry about, and what they care about. Most people could not dispose of their "things" tomorrow and still be happy or feel successful. When we allow things to dominate us, destruction is imminent.

From God's perspective, no human owns anything. God owns the whole universe; we are simply managing His property. We are stewards. Jesus was concerned that we be wise and compassionate stewards; He told two parables to illustrate these points.

The Steward

The problem. The steward in this parable was the manager of the owner's business, but he had squandered the owner's possessions. He may have wasted his master's wealth by excessive spending or by neglecting the duties of management. We cannot prove from the text that he was dishonest, although he is often called "the unjust steward."

Basically, he was lazy. His first reaction to being fired bears that out: "What shall I do, since my master is taking the stewardship away from me? I am not strong enough to dig; I am ashamed to beg."

The plan. The steward devised a plan that would benefit all who were involved. He let some debtors change their bills so they would pay only a part of what was owed. One paid fifty percent; another paid eighty percent. The steward thought those debtors would be grateful to him and would help him when he was out of a job.

Many students think this was a thoroughly dishonest trick, the steward gaining some advantage for himself at the owner's expense. They point out that the owner praised the steward's shrewdness, not his honesty. But obviously the owner knew what was done. If it was crooked, why didn't he have the steward put in prison instead of praising him? There are several ways to understand the story without accusing the steward of gross dishonesty.

1. Possibly the steward himself made up the difference with his own funds so that these people would be indebted to him. That seems unlikely, though. If he had enough money to do that, why was he so worried about losing his job?

2. These debts may have been uncollectible, soon to be written off. Any businessman can understand the wisdom of settling for less than the full amount in such cases. Partial payment is better than none.

3. The most probable explanation is that the steward had been working on a commission basis, and the amount he told the debtors to mark off was the amount of his own commission. By not charging a commission, he was making those people owe him a favor. Thus the owner, the steward, and the debtors all benefited.

The challenge. After Jesus told this parable, He made the significant comment that we read in Luke 16:8, 9:

> For the sons of this age are more shrewd in relation to their own kind than the sons of light. And I say to you, make friends for yourselves by means of the Mammon of unrighteousness; that when it fails, they may recieve you into the eternal dwellings.

He said that non-Christians (sons of this age) are keen enough to use some of their income for other non-Christians (their own kind) and thus both they and the others are benefited.

Jesus challenged Christians (sons of light) to do the same. We are to use our income for others, especially for our own kind, our fellow Christians, those of the household of faith (Galatians 6:10). If we do, those who precede us to Heaven (the eternal dwellings) will welcome us with gratitude.

It is a tragedy when pagans manage their possessions to fulfill their purposes better than the children of God do to fulfill God's purposes. We should use our possessions in such a way that our unity with one another will be tightened. There are many ways to accomplish this.

1. We can financially support the preaching of the Word both at home and abroad. Christians in the first century did that (Philippians 4:15; 2 Corinthians 11:8).

As we do that, those who are saved as the result of such evangelistic efforts will welcome us in Heaven.

2. We can also provide for the physical needs of our brothers and sisters in Christ. The early Christians were fine examples of such giving (Acts 2:44, 45; 4:36, 37; 11:29, 30). Paul spent a significant amount of time encouraging Christians to provide relief for the brethren in Judea who were hurt by the famine (1 Corinthians 16:1-3; 2 Corinthians 8, 9; Romans 15:25-27).

Jesus made it clear that our caring for others materially will affect our eternal destiny. Whatever we do or don't do for our brothers and sisters, He interprets it as done or not done for Him. Read this promise and warning in Matthew 25:34-45.

> Then the King will say to those on His right, Come . . . inherit the kingdom . . . for I was hungry, and you gave Me something to eat . . . to the extent that you did it to one of these brothers of Mine, even the least of them, you did it to Me. Then He will also say to those on His left, Depart . . . into the eternal fire . . . for I was hungry, and you gave Me nothing . . . to the extent that you did not do it to one of the least of these, you did not do it to Me.

One of the reasons for having gainful employment is to share with those who are in need (Ephesians 4:28). Christians should be good enough managers to make money so they can minister to others materially. Paul put it this way in his letter to Timothy (1 Timothy 6:17-19):

> Instruct those who are rich in this present world not to be conceited or to fix their hope on the uncertainty of riches, but on God, who richly supplies us with all things to enjoy. Instruct them

to do good, to be rich in good works, to be generous and ready to share, storing up for themselves the treasure of a good foundation for the future, so that they may take hold of that which is life indeed.

Our use of temporary possessions has eternal consequences. Jesus made this point quite clearly in the Sermon on the Mount. In Matthew 6:19, 20 we read:

Do not lay up for yourselves treasures upon earth, where moth and rust destroy, and where thieves break in and steal; but lay up for yourselves treasures in heaven, where neither moth nor rust destroys, and where thieves do not break in or steal.

Faithfulness in the use and distribution of possessions, Jesus said, is faithfulness "in a very little thing." It may sound strange to us to call our worldly wealth a little thing, for sometimes we do not look at our possessions as God does. He has given us all that we have (Luke 16:12), and He is testing us to see how we manage His possessions on earth. We will receive great blessings in Heaven as heirs of God and joint-heirs with Christ (Romans 8:17). God is watching how we manage things on earth to see if we can be entrusted with these eternal blessings in Heaven. If we do not serve God with our possessions here on earth, we show that we would not be willing to serve Him in Heaven.

Jesus also emphasized the truth that we cannot serve both our possessions and God (Luke 16:13). We must make a choice as to which will be first in our lives. We cannot serve both God *and* mammon, but we can live for and serve God *with* our mammon.

When Jesus made this point, the Pharisees scoffed. They had been trying to live for God and for possessions both (Luke 16:14). They rationalized their love for riches by saying that God gave them riches because they won His favor by doing right. They taught that God was punishing those who were poor. Their poverty proved that they were not righteous.

This same kind of thinking is still with us today. Many teach that God wants all His children to be rich, so if you have material possessions and riches, this is because you are especially favored by God. And if you don't, then there must be something wrong in your relationship with God. But that teaching is mistaken. God is the Creator of both the rich and the poor (Proverbs 22:2), and neither riches nor poverty is proof of God's love for us (Proverbs 30:8, 9). Those who try to make the poor feel inferior are reproaching God himself (Proverbs 14:31).

The Rich Man and Lazarus

The contrast. The contrast between the rich man and Lazarus in this parable of Jesus is striking. The rich man's purple robe was colored by a rare and precious dye, and his tunic of fine linen also was costly. It would take perhaps three years of a common laborer's pay to buy such an outfit, and this rich man dressed like that every day (Luke 16:19). His closets were full of expensive clothes; he gave costly banquets; he lived in a fancy home—quite a splendid life-style!

Instead of being covered with purple and linen, Lazarus was covered with sores. Instead of enjoying sumptuous meals, he was starving and dreaming about the bread that the rich man threw under the table (Luke 16:20, 21).

In those days, rich people wiped their hands on pieces of bread (instead of napkins) and tossed the soiled bread under the table. Some households had dogs that would lie under the table and eat the bread as it was tossed. The rich man's dogs were eating better than the beggar Lazarus. The rich man had daily feasts, while Lazarus was starving to death outside his door.

The dogs showed more compassion for Lazarus than the rich man did. At least they licked his sores, giving him some relief from his misery. It is a real shame that animals sometimes act more humane than humans do, while some humans act more savagely and ruthlessly than animals.

The death. There was quite a difference between the two men in life, but death is no respecter of persons. They both died. Perhaps Lazarus died of starvation, while the rich man died of a heart attack caused by overeating. What irony!

But they were treated differently in death. The rich man was simply buried, while Lazarus was carried to Heaven by the angels (Luke 16:22).

The reversal. Lazarus then became rich, while the rich man became poor. The rich man became a beggar, begging in his humiliation for a drop of water to cool his tongue. He now was miserable and desperate, much more so than Lazarus ever had been (Luke 16:24).

The rich man's neglect of Lazarus seems even more tragic when we notice that he says *"Father* Abraham." The rich man was a Jew just as Lazarus was! But the kinship had been totally ignored. And now the chasm that was between them could never be bridged. Who dug the chasm? In a real sense, the rich man dug it himself; and he knew it.

The plea. The rich man begged for someone to return from the dead to warn his brothers about their use of their possessions so they would not come to the same place of torment. His brothers probably had inherited this man's wealth; he wanted to tell them to use it to help others. He wanted them to notice and care about the beggars at their gates. He wanted them to open their checkbooks to meet others' needs. He wanted them to see that the closets filled with expensive clothes, the overflowing banquet tables, and the fat dogs were not worth a thing when eternal torment began.

Abraham's answer is a bit startling: "They have Moses and the Prophets; let them hear them" (Luke 16:29). The rich man said, "No, a person from the dead would be more effective" (Luke 16:30, my paraphrase). He knew that the Scriptures had not changed his conduct and that they probably would have no effect on his brothers, but he thought someone who returned from the dead would wake them up.

Abraham knew better. He knew that God speaks through His Word. He knew that if a man would not change when he knew of the authority and will of God, he would not change even if a dead person came back to life.

This should serve as a reminder to us. God means what He says in His Word, and how we obey Him will affect our eternal destinies. We cannot close our eyes and hearts to the needs of those around us and still expect to be welcomed in Heaven with open arms. If we fulfill all our selfish desires and bask in the luxury of many possessions while our fellowmen are starving about us, we cannot expect God to say to us at the judgment, "Well done." Think about it. How is your checkbook serving God today?

nineteen

He Will Come Again

Matthew 24; Mark 13

The look on their faces told me I had done the wrong thing. Some turned pale. All looked shocked. I had actually programmed some of them for heart attacks without realizing it.

It was Easter morning, and my sermon was relating the resurrection to the second coming. Dramatically I led up to the nearness of the second coming. I had one of the finest trumpeters in the area waiting in the foyer for my signal. Just when the people were sitting on the edge of their seats, breathlessly taking in every word about Jesus' return, I shouted, "And the trumpet of the Lord shall sound . . ." Then the blast of the trumpet was heard all over the auditorium.

I was afraid some of the people were going to faint. I had not intended for the experience to seem so real. Looking back on those immature, early days of my ministry, I realize that I should not have done such a thing to those people. But the shock that was reflected in their faces is probably pretty close to the way many of us feel about the second coming. Some of us seldom think about it, and some wish it would happen soon; but almost all of us would be surprised if it would happen today.

Such shock is really not misplaced. We know the second coming will be sudden and at a time when no one expects it. But of course we hope to be ready.

The Sure Sign

Many people expend much time and effort trying to figure out when the end of the world will happen and when Jesus will return. And I imagine all of us are curious.

Even Jesus' disciples shared this curiosity. Amazed at the beauty and seeming stability of the temple, some of them commented to Jesus, "Teacher, behold what wonderful stones and what wonderful buildings!" (Mark 13:1). But Jesus told them that the temple, even though it looked magnificent and permanent, would be destroyed.

The Jews thought that when the temple was destroyed the whole world would be destroyed. They felt that the world could not survive without Judaism. The disciples asked the logical question from their Jewish minds: "Tell us, when will these things be, and what will be the sign of Your coming, and the end of the age?" (Matthew 24:3). The disciples thought Christ's return and the end of the age would be simultaneous, but Jesus told them the events would be separated.

First, Jesus emphasized that they should be careful not to be misled or confused. He stressed that there will always be people claiming to be Christ, and there will always be devastating experiences (Mark 13:6-8). He warned them of the social upheaval and persecution that the new kingdom would bring because of its revolutionary life-style (Mark 13:9-13). He said the temple would be destroyed, but this would not be a sign of His second coming. It would happen when the

Romans would crush the city of Jerusalem. The Christians should flee to avoid that catastrophe (Mark 13:14-18). He told them those days would be extremely difficult, but they would not be the end of the world. Time would march on despite the destruction of Jerusalem (Mark 13:19-23).

But isn't there any sign that we can depend on to warn us that Jesus' return is imminent? Jesus mentioned only one sure sign—the sun and moon will be darkened, and the stars will fall from the sky (Mark 13:24, 25). When people see this sign, they will know that history has reached its end. Even the most isolated and primitive people will know that the end is near. But after this sign is seen there will be no time to get ready to meet Jesus. He will be here (Mark 13:26).

Jesus holds all of nature together (Colossians 1:17), regardless of how you understand the law of gravitation or the science of physics. He is the Lord of all the universe just as He is the Lord of all men. When He decides to "let go" of the forces of nature (sun, moon, and stars), He will be here; and time will be no more. We won't even have time to think about it; Jesus will be here.

He said this would happen "after that tribulation." *Tribulation* was a word used to describe intense pressure, like the pressure exerted to grind meal between two rocks. The destruction of the temple and the city of Jerusalem would be that kind of pressure (Mark 13:14-20), but still it would not signal the end of time.

It does mean, however, that we are now living in the last days. Jesus could return and the world could end before you finish reading this sentence.

Contrary to what some think, Jesus did not give us a blueprint by which we can figure out when He will return. He said He would come as a thief—unannounced, suddenly, and unexpectedly (1 Thessalonians 5:2, 3; 2 Peter 3:10; Revelation 3:3; 16:15).

We should not allow people to convince us that they have the time of Jesus' return all figured out, no matter how many charts they have drawn. Jesus did not know when it would be, and He was perfect. How could a man in his imperfection know what Jesus didn't? Jesus' words still stand: "But of that day or hour no one know, not even the angels in heaven, nor the Son, but the Father alone" (Mark 13:32; Matthew 24:36).

People today see all sorts of misleading signs. Some even move their families to a cave or a certain mountain to wait for the specific date that they believe Jesus will return. Their dates come and go; for according to the Bible, there is only one sure sign. When it appears, all of us will know it.

When He Comes

When Jesus returns, His light will be so bright that He will expose every sin with every excuse of the unsaved. The lost will run for the rocks and hills; the powerful and the puny, the rich and the poor alike will try to hide. The strong and the brave will become cowards (Revelation 6:15-17).

Jesus will return in the same way He left—in the clouds (Acts 1:9-11; Mark 13:26). He will come suddenly, and every eye shall see Him (Revelation 1:7). For once, every person on earth will see the same thing—even the blind. There will be no rose-colored glasses on that day, and there will be no debate about what is happening. No one will be puzzled; all will know. And we will either run *from* Him or *to* Him.

Jesus will come in all His power and glory. No evil will be able to stand His presence. He will come with the power to cast the devil, his angels, and his followers into Hell. He will come with the power to save the saints. He will come with the power to unite all His people, regardless of their separation in time and space. He will come with the power to begin a new heaven and a new earth.

When Jesus returns, He will gather all the saints (Mark 13:27). They will all be united and will live together in eternity. Our national, denominational, economical, and ethnic differences will be gone. Heaven will not be such a cultural shock to us if we will practice being the united family of God now on earth. It must break God's heart when we don't live together in mutual love, respect, and care; for that is the way we are to live in Heaven. Of course we cannot agree on everything, but we can be united in Jesus and treat each other with kindness instead of backbiting, criticizing, and promoting factions within God's family.

Jesus will gather the saints from everywhere, including those who have gone before us in death (1 Thessalonians 4:14-18). All the saints will meet and will break out in songs of praise (Revelation 4:9-11; 7:9-14; 11:15-17; 15:2-4; 19:5-7). We will be changed and will live eternally in the perfect environment of Heaven (1 Corinthians 15:51-54; Revelation 21:27).

What will happen to the unsaved? They will be gathered for eternal condemnation (Matthew 25:30, 41-46).

We will be in one crowd or another on that day. There will be no way to dodge it. We are either in God's army or the devil's. The uniform we are wearing when Jesus comes will determine in which camp we will spend eternity.

Be on the Alert

It is a waste of time and effort to try to calculate when Jesus will return. When the apostles asked Him again about the time of the restored kingdom, Jesus reminded them, "It is not for you to know times or epochs, which the Father has fixed by His own author-

139

ity (Acts 1:7). What did He say the apostles should do then? They should evangelize! (Acts 1:8). Jesus was warning them not to spend time making charts of the "end time"; He told them to get to work spreading His message of peace and love.

Jesus also told them to be alert, or to watch and pray, as the King James Version has it (Mark 13:33). He did not mean they were always to be on their knees or constantly sitting around gazing into the skies. He was talking about performance. Jesus has given us many responsibilities and expects us to carry them out. Watching properly involves working properly. And working properly involves living properly.

Jesus used a parable to emphasize this. He told of a man going on a journey and of the responsibilities he gave to those in charge of his property. He said the owner would return unexpectedly, so the servants must watch and not be caught napping (Mark 13:34-36; Matthew 24:42-46).

Jesus has gone away, leaving us to carry on His work on earth. He expects us to be continually vigilant, to be continually living as we should. For when He comes again, it will be too late to change.

Jesus told another parable to illustrate what will happen to those who are not ready—the parable of ten virgins in Matthew 25:1-13. There was going to be a wedding, and the virgins were expecting the bridegroom. But the bridegroom delayed his coming and came when they were dozing. Five virgins were caught unprepared and tried to do a last-minute catch-up, but it didn't work. They were left outside. Jesus will respond to such procrastination with, "I do not know you" (Matthew 25:12).

Jesus is going to return—that is certain. Are you ready? Be on the alert. Be doing the King's business. Don't be a dropout. Don't be out to lunch or awol when He comes.

twenty

The Lord's Supper

Matthew 26:26-29; Mark 14:22-25; Luke 22:17-20

Memo pads, bulletin boards, date books, grocery lists, notes on the calendar—all are reminders that we are forgetful people. If we aren't very careful, a birthday, an anniversary, or an important meeting date will fly right by without our realizing it. One time I was going to introduce my wife, and for the life of me I could not remember her name.

Jesus knew we were a forgetful bunch, so He instituted a meal to help us remember what He has done for us—the meal called the Lord's Supper or Communion. When He and His disciples were meeting for the Passover meal, He used this opportunity to institute a new ordinance for His church. It was the obvious time to do so, for what would happen to Jesus on the cross in a matter of hours would make the Passover meal obsolete.

Keeping the Covenant

The Passover meal was ordered by God to remind the Hebrews of their deliverance from Egypt, and the

Lord's Supper was begun to emphasize that an entirely new era had dawned. A New Covenant was to be put into effect. Like the former one, this covenant is an agreement, but not an agreement between equals. One person established the covenant and others accept it and abide by it as does the one who made it. The Hebrews made that clear about the Old Covenant when they said, "All that the Lord has spoken we will do, and we will be obedient!" (Exodus 24:7).

The Lord's Supper reminds us that we have entered into a covenant-relationship with God through the blood of Jesus. It reminds us that we too have promised to be obedient to the Lord. When did we make that promise? At our baptism. Baptism is our oath to obey God, and the Lord's Supper is our continual commitment to God and ourselves that we will not break our vow.

In the Latin church, both the Lord's Supper and baptism were called *sacramentum*. In military Latin, that term referred to the oath of allegiance that men took as they entered military service. Before taking the oath they were civilians. After taking it they were in the military. Their oath-taking was the point of transfer from one status to another. After the oath-taking they had a new commander, a new set of orders, a new living area, a new uniform, and new acquaintances and friends. Anyone who had not taken the oath was called a *paganus* which was the Latin for citizen or civilian.

It is much the same in the spiritual realm. Our faith and repentance are the means of changing positions, but it is our oath-taking event, our baptism, that is at the point of our changeover. At our baptism we receive a new commander (Jesus), new marching orders, (love one another, John 13:34, 35), new quarters (heavenly places, Ephesians 2:4-6), a new uniform (armor of God, Ephesians 6:10-17), and new friends (the church). At our baptism, we are transferred from one kingdom into another (Colossians 1:13). Anyone who has not been baptized is not in God's army, but is a citizen of this world.

For far too long we have failed to see our baptism as our oath to obey God—for better or for worse, in health or in sickness, in riches or in poverty as long as we live on earth.

In the Lord's Supper each Christian renews his commitment that he made in baptism. It is a renewal on a regular basis, so we won't forget our promise. We ought to participate in the Lord's Supper with a festive attitude, for we are reminded that we are a part of a New Covenant and free from the burdens of the old (Romans 7:4). That is truly good news!

We don't have to bring a young bull and sacrifice him as a burnt offering (Leviticus 1:2-9). We don't have to present a regular grain offering with oil and frankincense (Leviticus 2), a peace offering (Leviticus 3), or a guilt offering (Leviticus 4). We don't have to go to Jerusalem three times a year and spend a week attending a religious feast. We don't have to leave our fields idle every seven years. We are free to eat all sorts of food. We don't have to give a yearly offering for our sins or go through special ceremonies when we have certain diseases or are unclean because we have touched certain things or people. We should be celebrating every time we have the Lord's Supper because of the blessings of the New Covenant.

The New Covenant does not free us of all responsibilities, however, God calls us to grow up to His kind of actions and reactions. Review the Sermon on the Mount and note our responsibilities and the attitudes we are to have. Each time we partake of the Lord's Supper, we should commit ourselves anew to the teachings of the New Testament (which means New Covenant). The Old Covenant was mainly concerned

143

with practices, but the New Covenant is mostly concerned with the kind of *persons* we are becoming.

Jesus' Sacrifice

Jesus' sacrifice was universal: God so loved the *world* that He gave His Son (John 3:16). But His sacrifice was also limited: "That *whosoever believeth in Him* should not perish." Everyone is not automatically saved because Jesus died for the world. Jesus spotlighted that truth while instituting the Lord's Supper when He said, "This is My blood of the covenant, which is to be shed on behalf of many" (Mark 14:24). Why didn't He say "all"? Because the benefits of His death will be shared only by those who receive Him.

For this reason, our observance of the Lord's Supper should also remind us that there are many who are not saved; it should enhance our commitment to evangelism. Our thanksgiving for what Jesus did should motivate us to get going and win others to Him.

Forgiveness

The Lord's Supper also serves to remind us of the sins that have been forgiven (Matthew 26:28). The word *forgiveness* denotes complete release, deliverance, and dismissal. The root of the Greek word is "to send away." We are released from our sins when we receive Christ, because God does not remember them any more: "And their sins and their lawless deeds I will remember no more" (Hebrews 10:17).

God forgets our sins, and so should we. Many times we keep mulling over our mistakes, remembering our sins, and feeling guilty. We must realize that God has wiped our slate clean and has completely forgotten our sins. So instead of being weighed down at the time of Communion, we must allow God's grace to lighten our burdens and lift us up to live victoriously. We must remember the forgiveness more than our faults.

Every Lord's Supper should be a time of assurance for all Christians. The faithful Christian is not to live in fear but in confidence (1 John 4:17). We have no reason to shrink back at the thought of Jesus' coming again (1 John 2:28). We Christians must know that we are saved, and we can know it because of the promises in the Scriptures: "He who has the Son has the life, and he who does not have the Son of God does not have the life. These things I have written to you who believe in the name of the Son of God, in order that you may know that you have eternal life" (1 John 5:12, 13).

Hope for the Future

Not only is the Lord's Supper a reminder of the historical past (Jesus' sacrifice and our forgiveness) and our present status (we are saved), but it also gives us insight into the future. Jesus promised to eat this meal with us in the consummation of the Father's kingdom (Matthew 26:29). The Christian has an appointment to participate in a marriage banquet when Jesus comes again (Revelation 19:9). He has a fantastic future!

Until Jesus comes, we are to participate in the Lord's Supper (1 Corinthians 11:26; Acts 2:42). We are to keep our hands working in the present but have our eyes on the future. We must not allow our present surroundings to engulf us or allow our wonderful future in Heaven to isolate us so that we are no good on earth.

Unity

"For as often as you eat this bread and drink this cup, you proclaim the Lord's death until He comes" (1 Corinthians 11:26). We are not just to remember His death, we are to proclaim it. In partaking of the Lord's Supper we are proclaiming the reality and the results of His death.

Jesus not only forgave us individually and saved us individually; He also united us with all others who are forgiven. This unity is one of the important benefits of Christ's death, as Paul said in Ephesians 2:11-22:

> But now in Christ Jesus you who formerly were far off have been brought near by the blood of Christ. For He Himself is our peace, who made both groups into *one* and broke down the barrier of the dividing wall . . . that in Himself He might make the two into one new man, thus establishing peace, and might reconcile them both in *one* body . . . He came and preached peace . . . we both have our access in *one* Spirit to the Father . . . but you are fellow citizens . . . and are of God's household.

The Lord's Supper not only reminds us of the body of Jesus, it reminds us also of the unity that we have in His body today—the church. It is not surprising then that Jesus prayed for unity after instituting the Lord's Supper (John 17). Paul related unity to the Lord's Supper when he wrote, "Since there is one bread, we who are many are one body; for we all partake of the one bread" (1 Corinthians 10:17).

Regardless of the presence of the wine and bread in the Lord's Supper, we are not participating in the meal properly if there are factions within God's family. In the church at Corinth, Christians were worshiping separately with little regard for others, so Paul said, "You come together not for the better but for the worse. For, in the first place, when you come together as a church, I hear that divisions exist among you . . . therefore when you meet together, it is not to eat the Lord's Supper (1 Corinthians 11:17-20).

The instruction to "just think about Jesus and forget everyone else around you" is poor advice, for the

Lord's Supper is a family meal during which we are to discern not only the body of Jesus that was given for us (Luke 22:19), but also the body of Christ of which we are a part . . . the church (1 Corinthians 10:17).

The Lord's Supper is the focal activity of the gathered and worshiping church. It is an event that is to remind us of the unity we have with Christ and with His family. But it is not just a reminder; it is also an expression of that unity. The bankers and the paupers, the PhD's and the high school dropouts, the young and the old, the males and females—all are equal before God and share in the meal together. What a beautiful picture to see God's family gathered around His table for a family meal! What a time to pray for each other, serve one another, and be reconciled to one another!

When we consider the significance of this meal, observing it weekly is not too often. In fact, a daily sharing with brothers and sisters in Christ would not be too often (Acts 2:42, 46).

Let's not fuss about when we have the Lord's Supper, or how often, or whether we should use one cup or many. Instead, let's remember the covenant we have made, the sacrifice Jesus made, the forgiveness that is ours, the glorious future that is in store for us, and the unity of God's family.

twenty-one

The Greatest Serves

Luke 22:1-27; John 13:1-17

Bill Wallace, James Hainey, Larry Heister, Martin Horowitz, Ray Verville—I can still remember them. I can still picture their faces in my mind. Yet it has been thirty years since I have seen them or communicated with them. When I think about them, I meditate a long time; for I spent nearly eight years in the military service with them. We shared many experiences, and it was with some heartache that we separated. There is a certain longing peculiar to parting with friends.

Jesus had been through a lot with the particular men He chose to share His life with. And I am almost certain that His eyes must have been misty as He walked into that upper room to eat His last meal with these men. He probably reviewed in His mind the past three years; and as He looked at the face of each man around the table, He no doubt remembered the laughter and tears they had shared. He was soon going to die, and He wanted to spend this last evening with the twelve. "I have earnestly desired to eat this Passover with you" (Luke 22:15).

The Argument

The men had taken their seats around the table and were in the midst of the meal when it happened. A verbal free-for-all broke out. The disciples argued fiercely about which one of them was the greatest (Luke 22:24). The Greek word for *dispute* literally means a love of strife. The disciples were not simply passing the time with a friendly discussion. They were heatedly arguing and loving it. They had discussed the matter before (Luke 9:46-48; Matthew 18:1-5; 20:20-28), and were eager to debate it again.

Jesus earnestly desired to eat the Passover with His chosen disciples, but each of them earnestly desired to establish himself as a "big shot." Jesus was thinking of the cross He must suffer (Luke 22:15), but the disciples were discussing the crowns they thought they deserved.

The seating arrangement at the table may have sparked the dispute. It was customary as it is in some formal dinners now to seat the most honored guests nearest the host. Note how this custom is reflected in the teaching of Jesus in Luke 14:7-11. At the last supper of Jesus with His disciples, it seems that the most honored place went to John, who refers to himself as the disciple "whom Jesus loved" (John 13:23). If the host assigned places, all who were seated at the table would know who was considered the highest or lowest in his eyes. Perhaps some of the disciples thought they were seated in the wrong places.

Notice Jesus' startling announcement: "Behold, the hands of the one betraying Me is with Me on the table" (Luke 22:21). We cannot be sure that Luke tells these incidents in the same order that they happened; but if this came before the quarrel it may have helped to start it. The disciples began to discuss who the betrayer could be (Luke 22:23). Naturally all eyes automatically turned upon the one who was sitting in the lowest position at the table. He of course denied any intention of betraying Jesus. Possibly it was then that each disciple began to tell why he should have an important place.

Andrew may have recalled that he was the first one to recognize Jesus as the Messiah (John 1:40, 41). Peter may have reminded them that he had walked on water (Matthew 14:26-31). James and John may have talked about the times they and Peter had been with Jesus when the other disciples had not (Matthew 17:1; Mark 5:37). And so the dispute went on and on.

Before we shake our heads in disgust, let us think about our own attitudes. Are we more concerned about our status than our service? Are we more anxious to get our crown than to bear our cross? Are we upset when we don't get the honor and praise that we think we deserve? How do we feel about those who get to sing the solos in the worship service, or those who are asked to lead in prayer, or those who get their names in the church paper?

Jesus listened to their brag session and their disputing, and then He quieted them with a lesson about greatness.

The Comparison

"And He said to them, 'The kings of the Gentiles lord it over them; and those who have authority over them are called "Benefactors." But not so with you, but let him who is the greatest among you become as the youngest, and the leader as the servant' " (Luke 22:25, 26).

In that day the leaders of the people liked to be known as great. The emperors had their images imprinted on coins and had words under the images to tell how wonderful they were. Ptolemy I of Egypt was called "Benefactor"; Augustus, the first Roman emperor, was designated as "God"; Tiberius, emperor during Jesus' ministry, was described as "One who deserves to be adorned." These leaders wanted praise and demanded it.

Jesus said His followers were to be in direct contrast with such leaders. He said greatness came wrapped up in the package of willingness to do the tasks that were considered insignificant.

In those days young people were expected to be directed by their elders and to do humble and menial tasks. The aged were respected and honored as being sensible and wise. Jesus was not telling His disciples to act childish, but to be eager and willing to accept the petty and seemingly unimportant tasks that were assigned to servants and young people.

I have never noticed anyone feeling slighted because he was not asked to scrub out the bathroom sink and toilets in the church building, or cut the grass, or shovel the snow. But Jesus said such tasks are part of the life-style of those who are great in God's kingdom. Now who wants to stand in line to become great?

The Illustration

"For who is greater, the one who reclines at table, or the one who serves? Is it not the one who reclines at table? But I am among you as the one who serves" (Luke 22:27).

I have been in few homes that had the services of maids and butlers, but anyone entering such a home for dinner would certainly be able to tell who was the "greatest" in the dining room. The guests would be exquisitely dressed and using their best manners, while the butlers and maids would be dressed in their uniforms and running back and forth attending to all the needs of the guests. We would all say the guests were the prestigious ones in the room, but this was not Jesus' idea.

151

Jesus identified himself with the seemingly insignificant hired help who served others and then ate in a
corner of the back room. How about us? Are you an
employer that mixes with his employees? Do you ever
show up on the assembly line, the loading dock, the
press room, out in the field, or at the warehouse? As
parents, do you ever take the time to enter your child's
world? As a preacher do you ever serve a week in
Junior camp anymore?

Recently I attended a community breakfast where
the tables and chairs were to be put away after the
meal. All the men joined in to help with that menial
task—the doctors, the lawyers, the bankers, the
farmers—all except the preachers. They stood on a
balcony overlooking the work and talked among
themselves. Somehow I can't see Jesus standing on
that balcony. He would have been the first to grab a
broom and start sweeping. No lowly task would
threaten His greatness.

The Demonstration

Jesus not only taught about greatness; He showed
His disciples what it meant to be truly great (John
13:1-17).

In those days, the roads that people walked upon to
get from one place to another were quite dusty. When
it rained, they were quite muddy. The people did not
wear shoes like ours. Their sandal was a leather sole
tied to the foot with a couple of straps. It was easy to
untie the straps and take off the sandals when entering a house. At the door of each house was a large jar
of water to be used in washing the feet. A considerate
and wealthy host would have a slave to wash the feet
of his guests. This was done by pouring water over the
feet and wiping them with a towel. It was a slave's
job—the lowliest task of all.

But there was no slave in the upper room where
Jesus and His disciples had gathered. The disciples

knew their feet should be washed when they took their sandals off at the door, but they were more concerned about where they would sit at the table. One of those men could have volunteered to wash the feet of the others. Jesus gave them time enough to do so. But not one of them showed any interest in the type of servanthood that Jesus hoped would be their life-style.

So Jesus rose to wash the feet of His disciples. He did not do it to draw attention to himself. He did it because the men had a need; their feet were uncomfortable and dirty.

Jesus had only a few hours left to be with them; surely He would want to spend those last hours speaking about spiritual matters. Why would He waste time tending to physical needs? After all, their feet would just get dirty again, and they did not think the washing was important enough to do it for themselves. But Jesus was not just caring for their feet; He was caring for their whole beings. He knew they needed the spiritual teaching of this physical act.

Is it possible that we in the church get to thinking that our time on earth is too short to care for people's physical needs? Do we differentiate between spiritual and physical needs and neglect one kind? That was not Jesus' way. He used physical service in teaching spiritual truth.

Jesus never stood taller than when He stooped to wash the disciples' feet and wipe them with the towel. He even washed the feet of the man who would betray Him. It is one thing to minister to those who like us, but quite another to look out for those who don't.

When it was Peter's turn to receive that footwashing, he backed off and refused to let Jesus serve him. Peter's pride got in his way. Man's humility is seen not only in giving service, but also in being able to receive it graciously from someone else. It is the proud man who refuses help when it is offered.

Jesus made it clear that the fellowship He wanted with His apostles included the freedom to help when help was needed (John 13:8). The church is a family and should have that same type of fellowship. Members need to be open to give and receive. We must not let our pride get in the way; we must not pretend we have no needs that anyone can help us with. If we need financial help, for example, most of us would rather go to an impersonal institution than to let a brother or sister in Christ know about it.

Jesus was not setting up a specific ritual that was to be done by all people in all situations. When sandals become shoes and dirty streets become paved, the need for such a service ceases to exist. But Jesus was encouraging a certain attitude to be adopted by all people in all times, an attitude of unselfish service for others, even though it may be undignifed or humiliating.

What kind of activities today would exemplify the attitude that Jesus wants us to have? What is it that you don't like to do? What is needed, but degrading and repulsive to you? What is bothersome to you? That may be the very activity that is your "towel service."

For twenty years, I have consistently and conveniently forgotten to take out the garbage. It is such a disgusting and degrading task. The day I remember and cheerfully take out the garbage will be the day that I am serving my wife with "towel service."

God is pleased with those who keep a "towel" close by. His crowns are given to those who care.

twenty-two

Identifying Disciples

John 15

A few years ago, my family and I moved out into the country. We live close to a woods that has a small stream running through it. We have enjoyed hiking through the woods many times. Through this experience, I have become much more aware of nature and its ways.

I always knew that trees were different, but I had never really noticed in what ways they were different. With my limited knowledge, of course the trees all look the same to me in the winter. But when the leaves come out, I get a thrill out of going around and identifying the different trees.

I have made a few observations: Year after year the same types of leaves appear on the same trees. The leaves get their character from the trunk and root of the tree, and so does the fruit. I find it easy to identify trees by the fruit they bear. If I see apples on a tree, I know immediately that it is an apple tree. If I see cherries hanging from the branches, I know I have found a cherry tree.

Jesus showed no great interest in identifying trees, but He was extremely concerned that His disciples be identified as belonging to Him.

Jesus was participating in the Passover feast with His disciples. Soon He would be going to a garden to pray; soon He would be betrayed and arrested. He would die on the cross. He comforted His disciples by explaining that even though He would no longer be on the earth, His extended presence (the Holy Spirit) would live within them and give them the strength they needed to carry on their work (John 14). But having the Holy Spirit within them would not give them an all-inclusive, automatic identity; they still had the responsibility to bear the kind of fruit that would connect them with Jesus.

A group of disciples following a teacher around from place to place was a common sight in the first century; but after the teacher left, the group of disciples usually would break up or would find another teacher. Jesus did not want this to happen to His group; He wanted everyone to be able to identify His disciples immediately. He drew an illustration from nature—the vine and branches—to teach His disciples what was expected of them.

The Vine

Jesus said, "I am the *true* vine" (John 15:1). If He is the *true* vine, then there must be a false one. For centuries Israel had been designated as God's vine, (Psalm 80:8-16; Isaiah 5:1-7; Jeremiah 2:21; Hosea 10:1), and God had been designated as the vinedresser. God had benefited Israel with privilege after privilege. He even had asked, "What more was there to do for my vineyard that I have not done in it?" (Isaiah 5:4). He had expected Israel to produce good fruit, but she had produced worthless fruit; therefore God promised a change would take place.

Instead of planning for the people of the New Covenant to be connected to the Jews, God said they would be connected to Jesus, His Son. Jesus would be the vine that would carry the life to nourish and preserve the world from total destruction—the life that would be shared through His disciples, the branches.

Because of Jesus, something new would live in the hearts of men. When people were connected to the vine of Judaism, many of them lived for the institution, the rituals, the meetings, the synagogue, the temple, the sacrifices, and the law. Their religion was depersonalized. They were connected to procedures, not a person. The activities continued, but the inner thoughts and motivations of the people were not within God's will. Jesus wanted His disciples to know that they were to be connected to a person, not just another set of procedures. He wanted to change hearts, not compound rituals.

We Christians today must be careful that we don't revert to the ways of impersonal Judaism. We must realize that performing rituals and going to meetings are not all that is involved in our religion. Since we (as the branches) are connected to the vine, we are expected to look and act like Jesus (the vine) on the inside as well as on the outside. We are to become so intertwined with Jesus that it will be difficult to tell us apart from Him.

The Root and Vinedresser

There is no such thing as an independent vine. Jesus made that clear when He said His Father was the vinedresser or husbandman. God did many things for the vine: (1) selected the time for planting (in the fullness of time, God sent Jesus); (2) selected the place for planting (God chose Mary and Joseph and Bethlehem); (3) planted the seed (Jesus was conceived by the Holy Spirit); (4) cultivated the vine (Jesus did all in obedience to God); (5) and pruned the vine (Jesus suffered, Hebrews 5:8).

God is also the root of the vine; every vine has a root. The vine is dependent on the root for its characteristics. The vine displays on the surface the kind of life that is inside the root. This is exactly what Jesus did on earth (John 1:18; 12:49).

The Branches

If the purpose of the vine is to bring the life inside the root to the surface, then the purpose of the branches is to spread out that life. The branches are to bear fruit, the outer expression of the inner life.

Function. What is that kind of life? What kind of fruit are we to be bearing? The whole Gospel of John tells us of the kind of life that resides in the vine and is to be shown in the branches.

Jesus came to communicate God with grace and truth (John 1:1, 14). We also are to communicate God. We are to be God's mail to the world. What kind are we? Junk mail that is not worth opening? Some of us have truth, but are quite obnoxious about it. We spout the truth, but not in a gracious way. Or are we like blank pages? Some of us have all sorts of love to express, but have no truth to share.

Jesus had the presence of God within Him, the abiding Holy Spirit (John 1:32). We are to have God's presence within us, and we should be displaying it in our daily lives. Can others see God in us?

Jesus spoke of a new birth (John 3:1-8). As branches, we have experienced that new birth and are a part of a new family. Are we living like it? In John 4, we read that Jesus crossed barriers and accepted what His fellow Jews considered unacceptable. Are we breaking down barriers, or are we building fences?

In John 5:1-9 we see that Jesus was the healer. Are we seeking to heal the hurts of the world? Jesus said

He was the food that would nourish all (bread and water of life, John 6:51; 7:37). Are we saving and sustaining others with the nourishment of Jesus?

Jesus stated that He was light (John 9:5). Are we seeking to cancel out the darkness around us? Jesus gave sight to a blind man (John 9:1-7). Are we allowing Jesus to control our insights, and are we sharing Him with others? Jesus declared that He was the Shepherd who really cared for His sheep (John 10:11). Do we really care for people?

Jesus is the source of eternal life (John 11:25, 26). Are we taking our eternal life for granted, or are we still unsure of it? Jesus was (and is) a king (John 12:12-15). We share in His royalty. Do we act like it? Jesus was the lowly servant as well as the all-powerful God (John 13:1-5; 14:8-14). Do we have the humility to serve others and to show forth God's presence in our lives?

Future. What happens if a branch (a disciple) does not live up to its responsibility? It will be cut off from the vine and finally see destruction (John 15:6). The branch that does not function becomes dead wood; it is no longer of any use to the vine and therefore will be cut off.

Notice carefully that Jesus is talking about disciples of His who are not functioning. He is not talking about those who are outside of God's family. Outsiders are not a part of the vine, and therefore cannot be cut off. The application to us, then, is that membership in Christ's body is not an automatic and eternal guarantee of salvation. A Christian must act like Christ (bear fruit) in order to be identified as Jesus' disciple.

Purging or pruning. A branch that is continually producing fruit is improved by God so it can bear more fruit (John 15:2, 3). The New American Standard Version says God prunes it. The King James Version says He purges it. This is a more literal translation, for the Greek word means to purify or cleanse. The branch of a vine may be cleansed by pruning, but the purifying of a Christian is more internal. It is getting rid of whatever hinders spiritual growth or progress, whatever blocks the flow of life from the vine. Various attitudes and actions can do this.

To illustrate, three huge elm trees in our yard have died. The fungus that caused their death is carried by a very small insect. Once inside the tree, it spreads rapidly. It closes up the pores of the tree so it cannot get proper nourishment from the root—and it dies.

Blockages within us can also start in a small way and spread rapidly. But if we are bearing fruit, God cleans out those blockages so we can mature further.

How does He do it? He does it by situations in life (1 Peter 1:6, 7), by cleansing us of thoughts of self-importance (2 Corinthians 12:7-9), by the fellowship of God's people (Hebrews 10:23-25), by church discipline (1 Corinthians 5), and by the Word of God itself (2 Timothy 3:16, 17; 1 Peter 2:1-3).

Abiding. Jesus realized that He would soon be going to the cross. He knew that such a tragic and emotional event might cause His disciples to think all was lost. So Jesus many times said "abide." (The word appears ten times in seven verses, John 15:4-10.) He was saying, "Stick with Me. I am united with the eternal root—the supply source will never run dry. So regardless of how hot things get, stick with Me."

Abiding in Jesus is not some kind of mystical exercise. First of all, we must be united with Him (Galatians 3:27). When we are, He comes to live within us. As we allow His words to guide us, we are continuing to abide in Him (John 15:7). We continue to abide in Him as we obey His commandments (John 15:10). And we continue to abide in Him as we abide in His present-day body, the church.

Abiding in Jesus involves love (John 15:9, 10). Jesus often connected love with discipleship (John 13:34,

35). He showed what kind of actions emanate from the attitude of love when He washed the disciples' feet. Love is not some sentimental non-absolute that tells us to do whatever feels good. Real love involves concrete absolutes and is the fulfillment of all of Jesus' commandments (John 15:12). Every commandment in the New Testament is a command about love, for love does not do wrong to a neighbor (Romans 13:10).

The Results—Full Joy

The disciples (or branches) that abide in Jesus (or vine) are promised true joy (John 15:11). This type of joy is not the surface kind that gets squashed with the first setback. It is the kind that allows us to keep afloat, even though the winds and waves beat upon us in full force. We overcome them because of Jesus' presence and life-style within us. We have the strength and power of His Spirit, and we have His characteristics flowing through us and resulting in fruit. We also have one another. Each branch has the other branches surrounding it, protecting it, and encouraging it to remain on the vine.

Dark times may be ahead, the storms may be raging, the cross may be just around the corner, but full joy will keep us afloat!

twenty-three

A Matter of Life and Death

Matthew 26:36—27:54; Luke 22:39—23:48; John 18:1—19:37

Jesus had been rejected by nearly everyone at one point or another in His life. His hometown people had turned their backs on Him, multitudes of His followers had walked away from Him, His mother had tried to take Him back home, His half-brothers had not believed in Him. Now before the night was over all of His apostles would flee from Him. Only one had not forsaken Him—His Heavenly Father. But that too was soon to happen and Jesus knew it.

Jesus had just finished teaching His disciples and praying for them (John 13—17). Then He went into the Garden of Gethsemane to pray for himself.

The Garden

Jesus knew that He was to die for the sins of all mankind. He had foretold that several times (Matthew 16:21-23; 17:9, 12; 20:28). He had approached Jerusalem knowing what was going to happen. He had told the disciples about it very plainly, as we see in Luke 18:31-33.

And He took the twelve aside and said to them, "Behold, we are going up to Jerusalem, and all things which are written through the prophets about the Son of Man will be accomplished. For He will be delivered up to the Gentiles, and will be mocked and mistreated and spit upon, and after they have scourged Him, they will kill Him; and the third day He will rise again.

But when the time of torture and death drew near, Jesus asked God to detour the plan: "My Father, if it is possible, let this cup pass from Me" (Matthew 26:39). Why would Jesus want to bypass what He had predicted—indeed, what He had come to earth to do? With what was he wrestling in the garden?

Physical death is bad enough, especially death with all the torture of crucifixion. No man could face it without shrinking. But for Jesus there was more. There was the weight of sins not His own. There was the whole load of man's guilt. To take the place of sinful humanity, Jesus must suffer all that sinners suffer. He must be cut off from God—*spiritual* death.

Man's sin had earned the wages of death, spiritual death, separation from God. "But your iniquities have made a separation between you and your God" (Isaiah 59:2). That is what is meant by "dead in your trespasses" (Ephesians 2:1). That is what Jesus meant when He said, "Unless you believe that I am He, you shall die in your sins" (John 8:24). A person who dies physically while spiritually dead will live eternally in Hell. Jesus would cancel man's *spiritual* death sentence and save man from eternal torment. He would accept the wages of sin himself; He would voluntarily take our sins as His own. The prophets foretold that this would happen: "But He was pierced through for our transgressions, He was crushed for our iniquities; the chastening for our well-being fell upon Him" (Isaiah 53:5).

Jesus knew what would happen to Him on the cross. The only one who had never sinned would become sin (2 Corinthians 5:21). He would actually bear our sins in His body on the cross (1 Peter 2:24). Jesus knew He would be separated from God. Worse than physical death was that separation. He had never been separated from God, even for a split second. He *was* God (John 1:1). But He would be separated from God for the benefit of mankind.

Jesus prayed three times for such a cup to pass, but He did not give in to His feelings or His grief (Matthew 26:39). He knew that He would have to fulfill His commitment. So He handed His feelings over to God and asked that God's will be done.

I wonder how many of us could have done that. It is easy for us to rationalize and say that what *we* want to do is God's will. We get these feelings and think God has spoken to us. But how many times was that voice the voice of "inner self" rather than the voice of God? Confusing God's will with our selfish desires or feelings is a common fault of us humans. Since we can't become God, we try to whittle Him down to our size.

If Jesus had succumbed to His feelings that night in the garden, He would never have gone to the cross. How many crosses have we passed up because of our feelings that said no? We must follow Jesus' example and make decisions based upon commitments rather than feelings. Instead of following His feelings that said no, Jesus followed His commitment that said go. That is why He did not resist when the mob with their swords and clubs came to take Him away (Matthew 26:47, 50).

The Trial

It would have been nice if one person had stood up at Jesus' hearing to say a good word in appreciation of all that Jesus had done in the three years of His minis-

164

try, but no one did. The people whom Jesus had helped were either out of sight or were silent because of fear. Even the apostles had forsaken Him (Matthew 26:56).

Although no one said anything good about Him, it was hard to find anyone to say something bad about Him. Pilate pressed for some kind of charge against Jesus: "What accusation do you bring against this man?" (John 18:29). But all they could say was, "We would not have brought Him if He were not bad" (John 18:30, paraphrase mine).

Pilate saw through their facade and told them to take Jesus and judge Him for themselves (John 18:31). So the Jews drummed up a political charge, thinking that Pilate would pay attention to them then. But saying that Jesus was a revolutionary (Luke 23:2) did not impress Pilate either: "I find no guilt in this man" (Luke 23:4). Then the Jews finally spit out what was really bothering them—"He stirs up the people" (Luke 23:5).

The hypocrisy of the religious elite was made crystal clear during the trial of Jesus. After they turned Jesus over to the Romans, they would not enter into the Roman building "in order that they might not be defiled, but might eat the Passover" (John 18:28). So Pilate had to go in and out of the building; he would go in to talk to Jesus and then out again to talk with the Jews (John 18:29, 30; 19:4, 9, 13).

What a sad perversion of religion! These religious men did not want to touch Gentile property that would make them religiously unclean and keep them from partaking of the Passover. They took many pains to keep their outsides clean, but their insides were filled with schemes of murder. They were more concerned about keeping up appearances than with cleaning up their attitudes. They were more concerned about a perfect attendance record at a religious meeting than about inner righteousness and seeing that justice prevailed. What a farce their religion was!

In order to get rid of Jesus, His enemies lied, blasphemed, and murdered. Yet they would enter into their religious observances, pretending that they were "holy" people and that all was well between them and God.

Do we ever act that way? Do we ever disregard the mistreatment of a fellow man and at the same time maintain perfect attendance at our rituals? Do we ever spread false gossip about someone during the week and then praise God with the same mouth on Sunday? Are we peacemakers while worshipping, but soon afterwards destroyers of the peace by being unkind, critical, or demanding? We may say we would have never treated Jesus so terribly, but we must remember that how we treat others is how we are treating Him (Matthew 25:31-40).

Pilate declared that Jesus had no guilt, so he tried to maneuver His release. It was customary to release one prisoner of the Jews' choice at the Passover feast. Pilate gave them a choice between the mild, compassionate Jesus and Barabbas, a notorious robber, murderer, and insurrectionist (Luke 23:19, John 18:40). Pilate must have thought they would choose Jesus, but Pilate had misjudged how deep hatred could run and how violent the envious could become.

The "religious" people chose to release Barabbas—the sinner over the saint, the man over God-in-flesh, the thief over the truth, the crook over the Christ. And the chief priests and elders persuaded the lay people (the multitudes) to ask for Barabbas' release and for Jesus' death (Matthew 27:20).

Pilate could hardly believe the choice they had made. Even though a pagan, he knew it was terribly unjust to kill an innocent man. So he tried another approach. If they saw this man tortured, he thought, their thirst for blood and revenge would be satisfied, and they would allow Jesus to be freed. He had Jesus whip-lashed severely (John 19:1). The soldiers mocked Him and put thorns upon His brow. Pilate then brought Jesus out for the people to see, hoping their hearts would melt. He said, "Behold, the man" (John 19:5).

Instead of crying out for clemency, the people cried out for His crucifixion. Pilate was reluctant; he could find no fault in Jesus. He made further efforts to have Him released (John 19:12; Luke 23:20-22), but the Jews threatened him: "If you release this Man, you are no friend of Caesar; everyone who makes himself out to be a king opposes Caesar" (John 19:12).

Pilate had been on shaky ground with Caesar before. He knew he was walking on thin ice in his relationship with the emperor. His political career might be finished if a group of Jewish leaders would go to Rome and report that Pilate was tolerating a rebel who claimed to be a king. To save himself, Pilate ordered Jesus crucified.

Before we are too hard on Pilate, we must search our own practices. Do we sometimes allow the crowd around us to weaken our convictions about Jesus? Do we turn away from Jesus in order to save our own face? We want to be liked and accepted, so we may not stand up for Jesus in certain issues at home, at school, or at work. Pilate's attitude lives on even today.

The Cross

The captain of the guard wondered what kind of man this was on the center cross. Crucifixion was not new to this captain, but never had he crucified a man like this. Other men had to be tied to the cross while it lay on the ground in order to keep them there while the nails were driven into their hands. They would scream, curse, struggle, or weep; but not this man in the middle. He lay on the cross, giving no resistance. He remained still while the nails penetrated His skin and the blood gushed out.

Crucifixion was the most disgraceful and cruel way to die. It was nine o'clock in the morning when Jesus was nailed to the cross. In the midst of His pain and agony He thought of others: "Father, forgive them; for they do not know what they are doing" (Luke 23:34). He looked down upon the crowd and saw His mother. He knew how devastated she must be, and asked one of His disciples to look after her (John 19:27).

Every breath Jesus took on the cross was accompanied by suffering—thirst, fever, dizziness, throbbing, swelling, burning. The experience was so inhumane that Roman law would not permit a Roman citizen to be crucified. Even the brutal executioners allowed a special drink to deaden the pain. Jesus refused the pain-killer, but later allowed a moistened sponge to be put on His parched lips (Matthew 27:34, 48).

As Jesus breathed His last, He cried out, "My God, My God, why hast Thou forsaken Me?" (Matthew 27:46). Separated from God, He died spiritually as well as physically. Thus He tasted death for every person who has ever lived on earth (Hebrews 2:9). Our condemnation became His; and because of His death, we can receive the gift of life (Romans 8:1).

twenty-four

Hope for the Skeptics

Luke 24:1-47; John 20:24-29

It was a lazy Sunday morning. I had awakened earlier, but had dozed off again when I heard my mother scream. I knew something must be terribly wrong. I missed most of the stairs on my way down. Then I saw Dad sitting in the chair in a slumped position. I felt a slight pulse and started rubbing his arms (in those days we did not know about hitting the chest). Within a minute's time, I knew I had lost my dad.

I continued to rub his arms for forty-five minutes as the tears overflowed from my eyes. I knew what the doctor would say, but I still was not ready to hear those words: "I'm sorry. He's gone." I watched the funeral-home attendants lay Dad on a stretcher, cover him, put him in the ambulance, and drive away.

I was just entering my teenage years; I wanted and needed my dad. I yearned for the ambulance to turn around and bring him back. But it got to the end of the block and just kept on going.

I went with Mother when she made the funeral arrangements and picked out the casket. The funeral was held on schedule, and I watched the casket being lowered into the grave.

As much as I wanted my father back, I would not have believed it if he had walked into the kitchen for breakfast three days later. I doubt that I would have believed my friends if they had told me they had actually seen my father and talked to him after the funeral. His appearance after his death would have had to be verified to me, even if he had told me before he died that he would rise again.

The Doubt

I am glad the New Testament writers did not cover up the reluctance of the apostles to believe the resurrection of Jesus, because I can know that they were much like me. They had seen Jesus' wounded body after His horrible beating. They had watched when He could no longer bear the weight of the cross. They had heard the sound of the mallet driving the nails into His hands. They had watched His body swing as the cross was lifted and dropped into the hole with a thud. They had watched as His breaths became shallower; they had seen His head slump. They had seen Him wrapped for burial and placed in the tomb. Their beloved leader was dead. All their dreams and hopes could not change that fact.

The disciples began meeting behind closed doors (John 20:19). They knew they were in potential danger, for whatever happened to a teacher could also happen to his disciples. That is probably one of the major reasons they all fled when Jesus was arrested in the Garden of Gethsemane (Matthew 26:56). They were living in fear now; they no doubt started at every step they heard on the stairs outside the room. Were the soldiers coming after them?

Then the women came saying Jesus had arisen! (Matthew 28:8). How could this be? The disciples' refused to believe them, even though they said they had actually talked with Jesus (Matthew 28:8-10; John 20:14-18; Mark 16:11). In fact, "these words appeared to them as nonsense" (Luke 24:11).

They saw Jesus for themselves, but even then they thought it must be His spirit (Luke 24:37). Jesus showed them His hands and feet and invited them to touch Him (Luke 24:39). Still they could hardly believe their eyes and their touch. The truth seemed just too good to be true. "They still could not believe it for joy and were marveling" (Luke 24:41).

We can all understand their feelings. Haven't you ever encountered such a tremendous experience that your initial reaction was, "I can't believe it"?

Thomas

One apostle, Thomas, was absent when Jesus appeared to the others the first time. John makes a special point of noting Thomas' absence (John 20:24). Thomas has often been designated as the doubting disciple, but we can see that all of them doubted at first. Some have suggested that the problem with Thomas was not so much his skepticism as it was his absenteeism.

Significant things happen in the togetherness of God's people that cannot happen to one who wants to be a "lone-ranger" Christian. The things that happen within the fellowship of a congregation cannot be really appreciated by just hearing a committee report.

The disciples tried to tell Thomas what they had experienced, but he did not share their enthusiasm. "He said to them, 'Unless I shall see in His hands the imprint of the nails, and put my finger into the place of the nails, and put my hand into His side, I will not believe' " (John 20:25).

It is interesting that the other disciples did not criticize Thomas' skeptical mind or his previous absence. They did not turn their backs on him. Apparently there were no under-the-breath innuendos or raised eyebrows to make Thomas feel that he would not be welcomed in the group eight days later. These men had been through a lot together; they would not allow Thomas' unbelief to cause a rift in their fellowship.

We can learn from this example that we need to be patient with one another. If people are afraid to express their doubts among us because we will cut them to pieces, then we may be doing more to keep factions alive than to keep the fellowship going. Do we really want people to say they believe something when they don't? Thomas felt that he could say to these men, "I don't believe you."

A positive thing about Thomas was that he was willing to stand up against the crowd. He would not allow their position to become his just to fit in. He would not pretend about his belief. He was honest.

If Thomas had said he believed when he didn't, he would not have been a firm witness later. He would have been tossed to and fro as a wave before the wind. Had he not admitted his doubts, perhaps he would not have received the evidence that grounded his faith. Because he was an honest seeker, he grew in both knowledge and faith.

I wonder how many times we sit in a Sunday-school class and clam up; we won't admit that we are puzzled about a teaching. The tragedy is that unless we get our doubts and questions out into the open, we may never be exposed to the evidence or explanation that can help us. If we all would demand more proof about what is taught, we might look at the issues more honestly. By further examination we could see if the teaching is really valid or if it needs to be changed, according to the Biblical evidence.

Jesus did not condemn Thomas for his hesitation. He could have given him a verbal tongue-lashing for not believing. He had told the disciples repeatedly that He would rise from the dead (Matthew 12:40; 16:21; 17:9; 20:19). But Jesus took time to share the evidence with Thomas.

It is not proper to try to force a person to decide for Jesus against his will or understanding. It took Jesus and the apostles a whole week to convince Thomas; it will take much longer to convince some people. Jesus encouraged investigation, and so should we. If we have the truth, it can stand the most rigorous inspection. We should not feel threatened by a demand for evidence.

Jesus offered Thomas the same evidence that He had offered the others: "Reach here your finger, and see My hands; and reach here your hand, and put it into My side; and be not unbelieving, but believing" (John 20:27). But it seems that Thomas now did not need to touch Jesus; He saw and he believed. That was another positive thing about Thomas. When he did decide, he did not hedge. He did not rationalize or think about how foolish he might look in the eyes of the others. He did not make excuses so he could hold to his former position and save face. He could have said, "I am just seeing things."

I think we should be calling Thomas "the ready disciple," not "the doubting disciple." He was ready; all he needed was the evidence. The other disciples were not quite so quick to believe when they saw the evidence (Luke 24:41).

The Belief

Thomas immediately exclaimed, "My Lord and my God!" (John 20:28). He realized that Jesus was the God of Israel, the one named in the Shema—the credal statement repeated in every synagogue service—"Hear O Israel! the Lord is our God, the Lord is one!" (Deuteronomy 6:4).

There is a modern notion that Jesus did not claim to be divine and that only in later years did the disciples think He was divine, but the Bible does not support that notion. Jesus did claim to be one with God. His enemies understood that. Jesus did not deny the claim, but justified it. He was the one whom "the Father sanctified and sent into the world," and He proved it by doing the works of God (John 10:27-38). Thomas knew Jesus was God. So did Simon Peter (Matthew 16:16), Nathanael (John 1:49), John (John 1:1) and all the apostles.

The apostles set out to tell the world about the divine Christ risen from the dead, returned to Heaven, exalted at the right hand of the Father, and ruling as Lord and Christ (Acts 2:24, 33, 36). At that message the men of Israel were pierced to the heart. They had killed the divine Christ! Now what could they do? (Acts 2:37). Peter told them how they could find forgiveness and turn to live new lives (Acts 2:38).

Have you ever been a skeptic? Have you disbelieved, rejected, and scorned Jesus? Know assuredly that there is forgiveness for you also, even two thousand years after the resurrection. And even though you cannot see the wounds in His hands and side, your faith is not blind. Your belief is soundly based on historical evidence, as the next chapter will show.

twenty-five

He Is Risen

Matthew 28; Mark 16; Luke 24; John 20

Two thousand years from now some professors in
the political science department of a major university
may write that President John Kennedy died from a
severe case of measles. And some people may believe
it, thinking anything written by a PhD must be right.
But those who consider the evidence of history will
laugh in their faces. Even after two thousand years
there will be reliable records of what happened.

No one today would get by with that measles story,
because some of the people who were in Dallas and
witnessed the tragic shooting are still alive. It was
much the same in the first century: no one could say
the resurrection never happened, for there were too
many people who had seen Jesus alive after His death.

Jesus rose from the dead! That was the message
that spread across the world in the first century. Peter
announced it to the Jewish masses (Acts 2:24; 3:15),
to the Jewish officials in Jerusalem (Acts 4:10; 5:30),
and later to the Gentiles (Acts 10:40). Paul proclaimed
it to popular audiences (Acts 13:33, to philosophical

audiences (Acts 17:31), and to political audiences (Acts 26:8). He mentioned it to every person or church who got a letter from him except Philemon and Titus. However, to Titus he mentioned the second coming, which affirmed his belief in the resurrection; and to Philemon he mentioned "confidence in Christ," which implied that Jesus was alive.

Why didn't anyone stop these proclaimers by saying, "We've got you now. You are basing Christianity on the resurrection, but we all know Jesus did not rise from the dead"? Jerusalem would have been the place to stop Christianity, if it was false. If anyone would have known the resurrection story was a hoax, it would have been the Jerusalem dwellers.

But no one raised his voice to dispute the resurrection claim. The Jews in Acts 2 didn't. The hostile leaders mentioned in Acts 3 and 4 didn't. The priests of Acts 6:7 didn't. Saul didn't. Neither did Felix, Festus, or King Agrippa. Another story was being told to explain the empty tomb (Matthew 28:11-15). Why didn't anyone confront the apostles with it?

There was overwhelming evidence that the resurrection was real. Jesus made himself known to many during the forty days after He arose. Years later, Paul wrote, "He appeared to more than five hundred brethren at one time, most of whom remain until now, but some have fallen asleep" (1 Corinthians 15:6). This was Paul's way of saying, "If you don't believe it, check it out. The people who saw Him are still around, and there is proof galore."

Since the resurrection could not be denied, the hostile leaders tried to stop the Christian movement by ordering the proclaimers to shut up (Acts 4:17, 18; 5:40). When that order was ignored, they tried to stop the preachers of the gospel by persecuting, imprisoning, and murdering them (Acts 8:3; 9:1; 26:10). If they could not change or deny the historical facts, they thought they could at least try to wipe out the reporters of those facts.

The Evidence

What were the evidences that kept the first-century people from denying the resurrection?

The life of Jesus. Unless we could prove Jesus was alive in the first place, we wouldn't have much chance at proving a resurrection. But Jesus was highly visible. He was not an underground figure. Outside the New Testament account, other sources affirm Jesus' earthly life—Josephus, Tacitus, Pliny, Suetonius, Andrian, Antonius, Lucian, Celsus, Julian, and other historians of the time.

The credibility of the New Testament account. There were many witnesses in the first century who could have challenged any errors written in the New Testament. The New Testament is not what the church *wanted* to believe, but the facts to be believed because of the evidence.

The reality of Jesus' death. Unless it can be affirmed that Jesus really died, we cannot affirm a resurrection. But the facts surrounding His death leave absolutely no doubt that it was real. He did not just faint. He underwent a scourging that, according to Eusebius, left a man's veins, muscles, and bowels exposed. Weakened after a sleepless, foodless night and that beating, He was nailed to a cross for six hours.

His enemies knew He was dead. They came to watch Him die and were not about to leave without being satisfied. A spear was thrust into His side for the express purpose of being absolutely sure. The disciples knew He was dead. The centurion, an expert on executions, knew He was dead (Mark 15:44, 45). Joseph of Arimathea knew He was dead (John 19:38); he would hardly be interested in providing a tomb for a live man.

Yes, they did indeed bury a dead man. In fact, they buried Him in such a way that He would stay buried forever. They wrapped Him up like a mummy along with a hundred pounds of spices. Try getting out of that!

The conduct of the disciples. Before the resurrection, every one of them deserted Jesus. Peter wouldn't admit that he knew Jesus, not even to an insignificant maiden (Matthew 26:69-75). But after the resurrection, he replied boldly to the most powerful group of men in Palestine when they ordered him to quit speaking about Jesus' death and resurrection: "We cannot stop speaking what we have seen and heard" (Acts 4:20). Every one of the apostles (except Judas) followed Peter's example. It is thought that each one was executed for his proclamation (except John, who died a natural death). Without the reality of the resurrection, it is highly unlikely that these men would have stuck it out as they did.

Some say the apostles *wanted* to believe Jesus had risen, and so they convinced themselves that He had. No, not one of them believed Jesus would rise again. In fact, they were reluctant to believe it even when Jesus appeared to them.

The historical changes. Look at the calendar. It is dated from the time of Jesus. People would not have changed their calendars on the basis of hoax.

Consider the existence of the church. It gathered its members from those same people who had said to Pilate, "Crucify Him." Many who became part of the church would be kicked out of the synagogue, disowned by their families, and discharged from jobs; yet the church grew by leaps and bounds. People who had formerly hated each other joined in loving fellowship. The power of the resurrection broke down many barriers.

Consider the church ordinances. They point to a literal resurrection. Immersion reflects the death, burial, and resurrection of Jesus and our own new life (Romans 6). The Lord's Supper emphasizes Jesus' death, but also the future and Jesus' return.

Even the day of worship changed. After the resurrection, Christians worshiped on the first day of the week instead of the seventh. The Jews would have utterly rejected such a change except for the fact that Jesus arose on the first day of the week. The gathering was a celebration each week because Jesus was alive.

Those who never questioned the resurrection. Jesus' enemies did not challenge the resurrection. The chief priests paid the soldiers to lie and say that the disciples stole the body, but they knew He had risen. King Agrippa, Pilate, Felix, and Festus heard about the resurrection and did not challenge it. Many priests believed and became Christians (Acts 6:7).

Paul heard about the resurrection, but did not believe it at first. When the risen Jesus appeared to him, Paul knew. Then he considered all of the learning and knowledge he had gained up to that time to be rubbish (Philippians 3:4-14). He faced death many times, but he was absolutely convinced that death for him would be gain because Jesus had risen. Such a devoted Jew and ardent persecutor of Christians could not be so drastically changed on the basis of a hoax.

Even the pagan philosophers in Athens did not all deny the resurrection. Some of them mocked, but some of them became Christians (Acts 17:18-34).

Many Jews around the world knew about the resurrection. Jesus arose during a major Jewish festival, when Jerusalem was crowded with Jews from every corner of the world. Many of them told of the resurrection when they returned home. When Paul preached in the various cities, no one denied its reality. Many rejected Paul's teaching about the temple and the law, but it is not recorded that they denied his report of the resurrection.

It is interesting to note that the denials of the resurrection come mainly from the philosophers and theologians of the modern era who do not believe that God created the world or is in charge today. It becomes logical to deny the resurrection if we have no belief in supernatural powers behind the world and our lives on it. But it is not logical to deny the resurrection on historical grounds.

His actual appearances. For forty days Jesus appeared to people in His bodily form. We don't know exactly how many people saw Him or where they saw Him. We do know about one crowd of five hundred men (1 Corinthians 15:6). Following is a list of His known appearances:

Mary Magdalene—John 20:14-18; Mark 16:9
Other Women—Matthew 28:9, 10
Simon Peter—Luke 24:34
Two men on a road—Luke 24:13-33
The apostles except Thomas—Luke 24:36-43
The apostles with Thomas—John 20:26-29
Seven by the Lake of Tiberias—John 21:1-23
More than five hundred—1 Corinthians 15:6
James—1 Corinthians 15:7
The eleven—Matthew 28:16-20
At the ascension—Acts 1:3-12
Paul—Acts 9:3-6; 1 Corinthians 15:8
Stephen—Acts 7:55, 56
Paul in the temple—Acts 22:17-21
Paul in prison—Acts 23:11
John on Patmos—Revelation 1:9-19

The Good News

Pharaoh's tomb is not empty. Confucius' tomb is not empty. Buddha's tomb is not empty. Mohammed's tomb is not empty. Joseph Smith's tomb is not empty.

Jim Jones' tomb is not empty. Mr. Moon's tomb will not be empty.

But Jesus' tomb is empty! He has risen! It is no wonder the early Christians could not greet each other with a simple "hello." They had to express the joy they felt in their hearts. They greeted each other saying "He is risen!" "He is risen indeed!"

Portions of this chapter were taken from an article by the author in *Christian Standard* entitled "He Is Risen! Or Is He?", April 15, 1979, used with permission.

twenty-six

The Task Before Us

Matthew 28:19, 20; Mark 16:15, 16; Luke 24:44-47

A Modern Parable

John woke up one morning with a splitting headache and a high fever. The doctor diagnosed the problem as being a terminal sickness. However, there was a drug that could totally reverse the sickness if applied within twelve hours. The doctor dispatched two of John's friends with these words, "Go to the drug store, get this prescription filled, bring the drug back, and give it to John by four o'clock this afternoon. Then John will live."

John's friends left without delay. On the way to the drug store, however, they noticed a luncheon special at the local steak house. Knowing that they had plenty of time to get the medicine, they took time out for lunch. They got the prescription filled and started back. The title of the afternoon movie at the theater on Main Street caught their attention. They had both been wanting to see that movie. Knowing they had plenty of time, they watched the movie for a couple of hours. As they were leaving the theater, they noticed a small child standing beside the curb. The little two-year-old had lost his mother and was crying. John's friends spent twenty-five minutes helping the child find his mother. What a good deed they performed!

As they were approaching John's house, they saw a short, gray-haired old lady standing by her old car that had a flat tire. Again the the fellows felt they should help. That good deed done, they got back in their car and continued to John's house, which was several blocks away. It was about five minutes to four, but they felt sure they could make it. Sputter! Shudder! Gasp! Oh, no! The car was out of gas. They left the car and started to run full speed to John's house. They arrived with the drug at John's house at eight minutes after four. But John was dead.

Why did John die? It was not the lack of medicine or even the irresponsibility of his friends that killed him, though these were contributing factors. Only one thing killed John—his sickness. It was terminal with only one cure, and the cure did not reach him.

People in sin are in a terminal situation. The Bible makes it clear that sin results in death. Sin kills. Sin has terminal consequences. But there is a cure. Jesus is the only cure for man's sin. But what if man does not receive that cure in time? Then Jesus is worthless to him, and man will die in his sin.

We might say, "But that is not fair!" Who is to blame? The Creator? The curse? No, the killer is the deadly virus of sin, which we chose for ourselves. God, the Father, has given us the cure and told us to go to the world with it. If we do not reach men with the cure, the terminal consequences that are built into sin will come to pass in the lives of those in sin.

Proclamation a Must

People are not automatically saved just because Jesus came to earth. He has to be known and received. The same principle holds true in the physical realm. People in many parts of the world are dying of hunger and live in barren lands, while we have to worry about eating too much food and gaining too much weight. We have much potentially productive land that we haven't even used for crops yet. Some farmers have to destroy grain because we have too much. But even if we have food enough to feed all the hungry of the world, that does not mean those people are going to start gaining weight automatically. We have to get the food to them, and then they have to receive it and put it into their mouths.

Haven't you heard people say, "If the heathen have not heard of Christ, God in His mercy will save them"? The Bible does not support this concept at all. If it were true, then the best thing Christians could do would be to "close up shop" and be silent. If people are saved *until* they hear, we Christians could save the whole world by being silent.

If people can be saved without knowing about Jesus, then Jesus should have come to earth and died in privacy, on an island by himself. Then everyone would get a surprise at death. Surprise! You are saved! Jesus died for you!

If people are saved when they have never heard of Jesus, then God did a very cruel thing by commanding us to go and tell others. Some would say that we are to go and tell about Jesus because Christianity helps people of other cultures to be more loving and considerate. But how can helping a culture improve for a few years be compared to the eternal damnation that those who hear but don't receive will experience? If that concept were true, they would be better off not hearing of Jesus at all.

The truth is, those sinners who have not heard are lost. Sin kills them. Proclamation of the cure for sin—Christ—is essential. Without it, a person cannot receive the cure.

It is no wonder, then, that Jesus came to preach (Luke 4:18, 31, 32). It is no wonder that He commanded His disciples also to proclaim the gospel:

Go therefore and make disciples of all the nations, baptizing them in the name of the Father and the Son and the Holy Spirit, teaching them to observe all that I commanded you: and lo, I am with you always, even to the end of the age (Matthew 28:19, 20).

And He said to them, "Go into all the world and preach the gospel to all creation. He who has believed and has been baptized shall be saved; but he who has disbelieved shall be condemned. (Mark 16:15, 16).

And that repentance for forgiveness of sins should be proclaimed in His name to all the nations—beginning from Jerusalem (Luke 24:47).

As the Father has sent Me, I also send you (John 20:21).

But you shall receive power when the Holy Spirit has come upon you; and you shall be my witnesses both in Jerusalem and in all Judea and Samaria, and even to the remotest part of the earth (Acts 1:8).

There are four activities involved in Jesus' commission to His disciples: Going into all the world, making disciples, baptizing, and teaching.

Going into the world. Some have observed that the verb form for *go* is really a participle in the Greek and therefore should be translated "as you go." Although it is a participle, I think our version is correct in translating it as an imperative. In this sentence the main verb is *make disciples,* and it is in the imperative mode (a command). When a participle is connected with an imperative verb, it also receives the imperative emphasis. Jesus is commanding us to go. It is not an option.

As soon as the worship service is over, we "go." The Christians' gathering is always followed by the Christians' scattering; however, too often we do not sense that our scattering is as much a command as our gathering. Perhaps over the exit of every church building should be the words, "Go into all the world," to remind us that we are to depart with orders.

Simply going is not enough. We can be in perpetual motion without much really happening. We must penetrate into all nations in our going. The word *nations* stresses ethnic groups, not just geography. If we scattered into every country in the world but evangelized only the white Americans there, we would not be fulfilling Jesus' commission. On the other hand, we could go to New York City and evangelize every ethnic group there; but we still would not be touching every part of the world. "All the world" refers both to geography and to all kinds of people.

Making disciples. We are to be going everywhere for the purpose of making disciples. But who is a disciple?

The word itself involves learning: a disciple is a learner. But being a disciple of Jesus is more than learning some facts about Him. Hostile rulers in Jerusalem were told about Jesus, but they did not become disciples (Acts 5:27-33). To be a follower of Jesus is to make Him our Lord—not only to learn of Him, but to obey Him.

Our task is to make people followers of Jesus by teaching about Him and modeling His life-style in our own lives. A person is not a disciple of Jesus unless he believes in Jesus, repents of selfishness, and starts to follow Jesus.

Baptizing. We are to baptize them, according to Matthew 28:19. *Them* refers to the disciples we are making, not to all the nations, believing and unbelieving. We are to baptize only those who decide to follow Jesus, those who believe in Him and repent of their sins. Perhaps we have been too quick to baptize just anyone. Jesus commissioned us to baptize those who are becoming disciples.

To emphasize baptism to the neglect of making disciples is not to obey His commission. We are to baptize only repentant believers. Without repentance and a determination to follow Jesus, baptism has not one bit of spiritual significance attached to it.

Let us not be so quick to baptize those who just want to partake of the Lord's Supper, to have their names on the membership roll, to go to Heaven, to please friends or family members—but have no desire to know Jesus or follow Him. To become a Christian is to be dedicated to making a change in one's life, a change that leads to Christlikeness.

When a disciple is baptized, God grants forgiveness of sins, the gift of the Holy Spirit (Acts 2:38; 22:16), membership in Christ's body, the church (1 Corinthians 12:13), freedom from the law (Romans 7:4), unity with Christ (Galatians 3:27), unity with all of God's people (Galatians 3:28), salvation (Mark 16:16; 1 Peter 3:21), a new birth (John 3:5; Titus 3:5), a resurrection (Colossians 2:12), death to sin and a burial of the past (Romans 6:4), freedom from sin (Romans 6:7), freedom from condemnation (Romans 8:1), and a life with Christ (Colossians 2:13).

Teaching. The responsibility is not finished by the disciple's entrance into the family of God. The newborn Christian is to grow up in all aspects unto the likeness of Christ (Ephesians 4:13-15). Just as we do not aid in the birth of a physically newborn baby and then leave him to his own devices, neither should we do that with a spiritually newborn babe in Christ.

Our follow-up teaching is to be inclusive—all that Jesus taught. The newborn spiritual disciple will not grow up into Jesus' likeness without the full and complete teachings of Jesus. True disciples will *want* to be taught all of Jesus' commands.

Yes, Jesus left us with an awesome responsibility, but He also left us with His promise to be with us. How often? Always. For how long? Even unto the end of the age. What a wonderful promise! God is taking the risk and entrusting the future of the world to our commitment.

The Commitment

The early church was committed to proclamation of the gospel—the carrying out of Jesus' commission. The Christians of Antioch understood the need of proclaiming Christ and sent Paul and Barnabas on a proclaiming mission (Acts 13:2, 3). The early Christians proclaimed Christ everywhere—in the temple area, in the marketplace, in the synagogues, by the roadside, in a chariot, in a house, by a river, in prison, in a lecture hall, in a ship. Proclamation was done by *every* Christian (Acts 8:4); and it was done *for* everyone—Jews, Gentiles, the well, the sick, the young, the old, the rich, the poor, the politicians, the priests, the widows, the handicapped, men and women, the philosophers, the guards, the prisoners, even governors and kings. It was done every day: "And every day, in the temple and from house to house, they kept right on teaching and preaching Jesus as the Christ" (Acts 5:42).

In the New Testament there is not one case of a person's becoming a Christian without proclamation of the gospel. The Jews were not saved until Jesus was proclaimed to them (Acts 2). The Samaritans were not saved until a refugee from Jerusalem proclaimed Jesus to them (Acts 8:5-13). The Ethiopian eunuch was not saved until Jesus was proclaimed to him (Acts 8:26-40). Paul was not saved (although blameless by the standards of the law, Philippians 3:6) until after Jesus declared himself to him and after Ananias shared with him what he must do (Acts 9:5, 6; 22:12-16). Cornelius was not saved until Jesus was proclaimed to him by Peter (Acts 10:34-48). The people in Antioch were not saved until Jesus was proclaimed to them (Acts 11:19-21).

It is interesting to note that Cornelius had a visit from an angel and Paul had a personal encounter with Jesus, but neither of them was saved by his supernatural experience. No one was saved *without* proclamation through another human person. God did not go to people directly and evangelize them; He used other people to preach and teach about Jesus.

The apostles and the early Christians did not stop with just evangelizing either. They continued in teaching, in exhortation, and in confirming the disciples that were made. They also wrote epistles to help them with their problems of growth and to give them guidelines to follow in their growth as Christians.

We are all farmers with Christ's seed, bakers with His bread, fishermen in His sea, shepherds with His sheep, wicks in His lanterns, tools in His shop, investors in His treasury, proclaimers of His Word, and ambassadors with His ministry.

When Bud Wilkinson was asked what he thought football had contributed to physical fitness in the United States, he answered, "Not a thing." A startling reply! He went on to explain, "There are twenty-two tired, worn-out men on the field who need some rest, while in the stands watching are fifty-thousand people who need some exercise."

189

We in the church can become like those people in the stands if we are not careful. Let us be certain that the majority of the church members are not sitting in the stands while a few are laboring to carry out Jesus' commission. Everyone is needed if the world is to be won for Christ and escape eternal punishment for sin. Let us not be lazy. Let us not procrastinate and act irresponsibly as did those friends in the parable at the beginning of this chapter. Let us realize that sin is deadly, and we are the only ones with the cure.

Portions of this chapter were taken from an article written by the author, "Proclamation," March 9, 1980, issue of *Christian Standard,* used by permission.

THE NEW LIFE SERIES

The books in the New Life Series take seriously the fact that Jesus came to give us new life. They take seriously the fact that the Bible is God's inspired Word for us and is "profitable for teaching, for reproof, for correction, for training in righteousness; that the man of God may be adequate, equipped for every good work" (2 Timothy 3:16, 17).

They take seriously the fact that every member of Christ's church, His body, is a minister of God. Many books are written in the language of scholars, but these books are written in the everyday language of the average person. They put the fruit of scholarship into the language of the layman to help bring people to the Lord and build them up in the Lord.

The authors of these books have tried consistently to bring together the meaning of the text and the application of that meaning in our current lives. They are interested in pointing the readers to the living and written Word so their lives can be changed.

We encourage you to put all the books of this series into your library and make time on your reading schedule for them. They can be read and studied individually or shared with study groups. Each book has an instructor's guide that can be purchased separately for use by a teacher to enhance class discussion and to provide ideas for learning activities and projects.

Books in the New Life Series are listed on the next page. You may order them from your supplier.

Up From Chaos
by LeRoy Lawson
A study of Genesis unlike any you ever saw before.

The True Life
The Only Way
by Lewis Foster
Twin volumes to deepen your appreciation of the
Gospel of John

After the Spirit Comes
by Roger Thomas
Tracing the dominant themes of the book of Acts

His Way
by Jack Cottrell
A refreshing look at the Ten Commandments and
Christian teaching on the same themes

His Truth
by Jack Cottrell
A profoundly simple presentation
of basic Bible doctrines

A Loser, A Winner, and A Wise Guy
by David McCord
A study of Saul, David, and Solomon

Divided We Fall
by James E Smith
Considers the fall of Israel and Judah

God's OK—You're OK?
by R. W. Baynes
Worship as a transaction between God and man

Why Believe?
by Richard Koffarnus
A study of apologetics